THE FORGOTTEN
LUTHER

Reclaiming the Social-Economic
Dimension of the Reformation

EDITED BY
CARTER LINDBERG AND PAUL WEE

Lutheran University Press
Minneapolis, Minnesota

The Forgotten Luther
Reclaiming the Social-Economic Dimension
of the Reformation
Edited by Carter Lindberg and Paul Wee

The photo on the cover shows Martin Luther's Community Chest, now located in the Luther Museum in Wittenberg, Germany. Photo is courtesy of Paul Wee.

ISBN 978-1-942304-17-3

Lutheran University Press, PO Box 390759, Minneapolis, MN 55439
www.lutheranupress.org
Manufactured in the United States of America

Contents

Acknowledgments

Above all we would like to thank the members of the Forgotten Luther Working Group for their commitment to economic justice and their willingness to commit time, talents and considerable energy to planning the Symposium. These leaders are from the Church of the Reformation (Lutheran) in Washington, D.C., and Good Shepherd Lutheran Church in Alexandria, Virginia: Al Anderson, Pastor Phillip Anderson, Scott Binde, Karen Cowden, John Hagood, Russell Hillberry, Pastor Jeanette Leisk, Amy Northcutt, and Kathryn Tobias. Special thanks go to the treasurer of the Church of the Reformation, Ms. Suzanne Hazard.

Providing an ecumenical dimension to the study of Luther's social reforms was a group of actively retired church leaders from the Goodwin House in Falls Church, Virginia: Bishop Ted Eastman (Episcopal), Pastor Jeanne McKenzie (Presbyterian), Dr. Loren Mead (Episcopal), Al Anderson (Lutheran) and Dr. Tony Tambasco (Roman Catholic). This group noted the striking similarity in the views of Martin Luther and Pope Francis on the need to address the structural causes of hunger and poverty. A letter from the group, calling on the Pope "to facilitate an ecumenical conversation on the stewardship of economic life to address these critical issues," was hand-delivered to Pope Francis during his 2015 visit to the United States.

We would also like to express our gratitude to the leaders of the global study project, *Radicalizing Reformation—Provoked by the Bible and Today's Crises,* in particular the noted Lutheran theologian, Dr. Ulrich Duchrow of Heidelberg, Germany. Geared to the 500th anniversary of the Reformation, this multi-national study is based on the conviction that "the central biblical message is about God`s compassion and justice and, therefore, about liberation from oppression and injustice." The North American coordinator of the project is Dr. Karen Bloomquist, former director of the Department for Theology and Studies of the Geneva-based Lutheran World Federation. For further information on this global study project, see: www.radicalizing-reformation.com. The *Radicalizing Reformation* project has already produced five volumes of articles in English and German (see *Suggestions for further reading*). These are available for congregations and institutions through the LIT Verlag in Germany (vertrieb@lit-verlag.de; www.lit-verlag.de). An all-English volume is available on Amazon.com. We are grateful to the LIT Verlag for permission to reproduce the article by Cynthia Moe-Lobeda and to the U.S.-based *Dialog: A Journal of Theology,* (Rev. Dr. Kristin Johnston Largen, editor, Vol. 55, Issue 1, Online ISSN: 1540-6385, copyright courtesy of Wiley Editing Services), for permission to reproduce the article by Samuel Torvend.

We are most grateful for financial support for this project from the Metropolitan Washington, D.C. Synod of the Evangelical Lutheran Church in America (ELCA), in particular: Bishop Richard Graham; the Global Mission Committee of the Synod, led by Rev. Bob Allard; the Embassy of the Federal Republic of Germany; Pastor Connie Miller and St. Luke Lutheran Church in Silver Spring, Maryland; the ELCA's World Hunger Education unit; as well as from a number of community organizations, committed congregations, and individuals.

The release of this book in such a timely fashion owes a huge debt of gratitude to Lutheran University Press and its publisher, Karen Walhof. It was a pleasure for us to work with someone so competent and congenial.

Finally, we want to thank the Church of the Reformation, located on Capitol Hill in Washington, D.C., for hosting the Forgotten Luther Symposium. The congregation, located a block from the U.S. Capitol and the Supreme Court, understands its vocation to bring the gospel of Christ to bear on the critical issues of the day. We are admittedly biased, but the three of us were pleased to serve this congregation as its senior pastors and to work together to carry out the Forgotten Luther Symposium.

Paul Wee (1994-1999)
Conrad Braaten (2000-2011)
Michael Wilker (2011-present)

Abbreviations

Luther's Works, (Minneapolis/St. Louis: Fortress/Concordia, 1955ff.) Abbreviated LW, volume, page(s); (e.g., LW 1:1)

D. Martin Luthers Werke (Weimar: Böhlau, 1883ff). Abbreviated WA: volume, page(s), lines(s); (e.g., WA 1:1,1)

The Small Catechism and The Large Catechism in Robert Kolb & Timothy Wengert, eds., *The Book of Concord: The Confessions of the Evangelical Lutheran Church* (Fortress, 2000). Abbreviated BC page(s)

The cover of Luther's
"Ordance for a Common Chest"

Introduction

Paul Wee and Conrad Braaten

> [I]t is a question of a fair balance between your present abundance and their need, so that their abundance may be for your need, in order that there may be a fair balance. As it is written, "The one who had much did not have too much, and the one who had little did not have too little.
>
> St. Paul in 2 Corinthians 8: 13-15

> God is the kind of Lord who does nothing but exalt those of low degree and put down the mighty from their thrones, in short, break what is whole and make whole what is broken.
>
> Martin Luther, LW 21:299-300

Discovering the Forgotten Luther

The story of this volume has grown out of the life of congregations rooted in the heritage of the Reformation. It began when some members experienced the painful truth that they could no longer adequately feed and care for their families. They felt some shame that in this "land of opportunity" they were not able to maintain an income level sufficient to keep them from falling over the edge. Others who were not experiencing hunger or feeling the effects of poverty, but who were aware of the pain of their sisters and brothers, also began asking how it was possible that so many in our society were being forced to suffer the insecurities that come from a declining income.

As followers of Jesus Christ, they had another question: How does such income disparity mesh with the biblical call to share the wealth of God's creation with equity? How does the existence of extreme wealth alongside of hunger and poverty—in our country and in our world— mesh with St. Paul's admonition to the Corinthians to strike a "fair balance between your present abundance and their need"?

The determination to respond to this imbalance gathered momentum as church members, aware of a number of successful efforts to reduce poverty levels and stimulated by the work of ELCA World Hunger and other ministries, concluded that they needed to address, not simply the *effects* of hunger and poverty (through, for example, food distribution programs), but also the systemic factors that *cause and perpetuate* hunger and poverty.

What these congregations discovered—and what any concerned congregation will discover in the materials of this publication—is startling. In a word, they were surprised to discover the significant resources within their own Reformation heritage for dealing with these issues. Many were shocked to learn that, from his earliest days in Wittenberg when he saw the adverse effects of the new market economy on the common people and was overwhelmed by the sheer number of beggars on the streets, Martin Luther had committed such a great deal of theological energy and passion to this issue.

> The poor are defrauded every day, and new burdens and higher prices are imposed. They all misuse the market in their own arbitrary, defiant, arrogant way, as if it were their right and privilege to sell their goods as high as they please without criticism (from The Large Catechism).

Another surprise followed. It came when lay people who knew something about economic forces came to the realization that, in spite of the vast differences between Luther's time and our own, many of the most basic principles at work—both theological and economic—remain the same.

Because this significant aspect of the Reformer's thought and activity has, in the view of the contributors, been largely neglected in Christian education—in Sunday school, confirmation, and even college and seminary curricula—we've called this simply *The Forgotten Luther: Reclaiming the Social-Economic Dimension of the Reformation.*

The "Forgotten Luther" Symposium

It was this discovery, namely that Martin Luther maintained a passionate and nearly lifelong commitment to addressing the *systemic* causes of hunger and poverty, that led our working group to ask how these findings might be discussed and tested through exposure to a wider audience. The result was the creation of the Forgotten Luther

Symposium, a two-day gathering of clergy and laity held at the Church of the Reformation in Washington, D.C., in November 2015. The symposium featured the original music of the congregation's acclaimed composer and Director of Music, Paul Leavitt, and the Reformation Choir. A forty-minute drama, *The Forgotten Luther,** was performed, setting the historical context for the lectures and discussion. The symposium also served a dinner of "Bier und Brats," sauerkraut, and fried potatoes to give the entire discussion the atmosphere of Luther's Wittenberg.

Publishing the symposium presentations in this volume is the result of requests from many of the people who attended the symposium. With the help of a transition article by Dr. Ryan Cumming, of ELCA World Hunger, a ministry of the Evangelical Lutheran Church in America (ELCA), the volume moves from the presentations to a number of questions for discussion by concerned groups within the church.

A Challenge to the Laity

This study is geared to the lay people within every congregation who are committed to the mission of the church. It assumes not only that they are prepared to follow Christ's call to love the neighbor, but also that they are willing to give tangible expression to that calling through use of their talents, experiences, and knowledge. Indeed, our experience has confirmed the fact that congregations are filled with people who are "economics savvy" and prepared to use their knowledge in addressing the complex causes of the present income disparity.

Because Luther himself viewed the means to be employed in addressing hunger and poverty to be in the area of Christian freedom, in which followers of Christ use their reason to work out ways in which love of the neighbor might be expressed, those who participate in this study are asked to do the same: welcome creativity, be open to learning, and avoid partisanship. There was for Luther—and should be also for us today—no single, biblically-mandated economic model, no direct line from the biblical witness to any specific economic institution or system. To claim such, as some have done, is to confuse law with gospel. Rather, our discussion is in the realm of Christian freedom. It asks how we might use our God-given creativity and reason to express what St. Paul calls "faith active in love."

---

* The *Forgotten Luther* drama is easily adaptable to a variety of public or congregational settings and can be secured without fee at drpaulwee@gmail.com.

The Contributors to this Volume

All of the contributors to this volume orient their remarks within the framework of the Reformation heritage and its central teaching on justification by grace through faith. Seeking to recover a dimension of that heritage that has often been overlooked, they draw some provocative implications for the contemporary life and mission of the church.

Conrad Braaten

A pastor of the Evangelical Lutheran Church in America, Braaten is responsible for initiating the "Forgotten Luther" project. A retired (2012) senior pastor of the Church of the Reformation on Capitol Hill, he also worked on the staff of the ELCA Division for Congregational Life in the program areas of Urban Ministry and Congregational Social Ministry, and for over a decade was a member of the U.S.A. Committee of the Lutheran World Federation's Caribbean-Haiti Program. He has coordinated and led over twenty-five educational immersions to countries in the Caribbean, Central America, and South America. He has written on biblical and theological themes and continues to engage in programs designed to equip pastors and lay people in methods of advocacy on behalf of those who have been denied justice

Carter Lindberg

Among the respected scholars who contributed to this volume, it is Carter Lindberg who occupies a special place. His breakthrough book, *Beyond Poverty: Reformation Initiatives for the Poor* (Fortress Press, 1993), established the foundation for the study of Luther's social reforms. In fascinating detail, Lindberg tells the powerful, but strangely ignored story of how Luther worked with the civil authorities to create the "common chest" *(die gemeinsame Kasten)*, instigating a revolution that would spread throughout Germany and would eventually influence the structures of economic life in Western Europe and Scandinavia as well.

Lindberg makes it clear that at the heart of this change in the economic structure was Luther's understanding of justification by grace through faith alone. The free gift of God's grace undercuts the medieval notion that the vast imbalance in the distribution of wealth is part of God's plan for the creation. At the same time the free grace of God liberates for action to free the neighbor from the bonds of hunger and poverty.

Samuel Torvend

On the face of it, one might think Samuel Torvend's contribution, "Greed Is an Unbelieving Scoundrel," to be a conventional diatribe against one of the most ubiquitous of the seven deadly sins. Indeed, Luther often railed against personal greed, how "skillfully Sir Greed can dress up to look like a pious man," from the pulpit of St. Mary's Church on the *Marktplatz* in Wittenberg. But neither Luther nor Torvend thought that a sermonic tongue-lashing was sufficient. For both, the more sinister manifestation of greed is its expression in systems of power, in the rules of trade, the regulations of the banking industry, and the policies of corporations and governments. After reading Torvend's chapter—and his stimulating study, *Luther and the Hungry Poor: Gathered Fragments* (Fortress, 2008)—the reader might well receive fresh and surprising insight into what the evangelical Reformation was all about.

Cynthia Moe-Lobeda

In her lecture, in which she calls on the churches of the Reformation to drink from "the wellsprings of our radical heritage," Cynthia Moe-Lobeda demonstrates why she has become one of the most original thinkers in theology today. Those who have read her stimulating study, *Resisting Structural Evil: Love as Ecological-Economic Vocation* (Fortress, 2013), will clearly have braced themselves for a reading of "The Subversive Luther" with its clear implication for how the church works out its calling in the world. She minces no words in demonstrating how a tradition born in resistance has become "tamed" by an uncritical accommodation to the prevailing "power alignments and their ideological underpinnings." Where churches in the Reformation tradition have rightly given attention to the centrality of God's grace, they have, she claims, neglected the call to love the neighbor by resisting systems that exploit the poor. She notes that for Luther the "indwelling of Christ" is hardly a flight into personal spirituality; rather, it is a call to risk one's own life for the sake of the neighbor.

Jon Pahl

If you have come out of a confirmation tradition based on the reading and reciting of Luther's Small Catechism, you need to prepare yourself for Jon Pahl's scholarly and provocative second look at this tradition. Both the Small Catechism and its more elaborate companion, the Large Catechism, need to be read with new eyes, capable of seeing the economic context in which they were written and the exploitative practices to which they were addressed. When such a re-reading happens, readers might discover something about their own world—and about their own hearts and minds—for which they were not prepared. Luther's explanation of the seventh commandment, in both catechisms, for example, addresses not only the human propensity to take what belongs to others. It addresses systems of economic and social life that exploit the most vulnerable members of society. Pahl then explores two structural models designed to protect the most vulnerable that are rooted in Luther's thinking, the one emphasizing the God-given role of the state in insuring the well-being of the citizenry, the other emphasizing the important role of voluntarism and its agencies that serve the poor. These models, Pahl claims, are not mutually exclusive but complementary. To understand this, he claims, requires an economic reading of Luther's catechisms.

Tim Huffman

Affirming and then building on the preceding chapters, Huffman, provides us with two fascinating images of Luther's oft-forgotten role in economic life. The first is the simple fact that Luther was engaged in concrete economic realities throughout his life—first as a child exposed to the problems of copper miners at his father's smelter in the town of Mansfield, and later, at the end of his life, as a respected leader seeking to mediate a dispute between mine owners and workers in the same town. In between we see his attack on the practice of lending money to the poor with interest (usury), his writing and speaking out against the sale of indulgences, and his initiative in establishing rules for wealth-sharing that he considered to be more in keeping with the biblical call to share the wealth of the earth with equity.

The second image is even more startling. It is the portrayal of the global economic ramifications of Luther's teachings in the liberation theologies that have, in previous decades, rocked the social, economic, and political foundations of several Latin American countries. It is highly ironic, claims Huffman, that it has been above all Roman Catholic leaders who have seized on the work of the Protestant Reformer in their quest to help equalize the playing field by encouraging a "preferential option for the poor" to transform economic conditions.

Critical to grasping the radical nature of Luther's reform is, for

Huffman, an understanding of his insistence on the centrality of justification by grace through faith. It is God's freely given grace in Jesus Christ that frees us and motivates us to engage in actions that serve the liberation of the neighbor. What is needed, Huffman claims, is the rediscovery of the integral relationship between justification and justice.

Ryan P. Cumming

If such a rediscovery of the relationship between justification and justice is to take place among us, claims Ryan Cumming, it will require a major shift in perspective. It will require a "new vision." Cumming assumes that churches born of the Reformation are in fact committed to achieving a "fair balance" between the abundance of the few and needs of the many. They do not want people to suffer. Yet their good intentioned actions might lead, ironically, to precisely the opposite result. Food distribution programs, for example, might become "toxic" if they simply create dependency and self-reliance. They might actually serve to reinforce the structures of dependency. To avoid this "a dramatic change in perception" is required. Cumming clearly believes that such a change is not out of the reach of many gifted congregations. Required are "new eyes" to see not only the complex "root ball" of causes of hunger and poverty within the systems of economic life, but a new lens through which one can rediscover the calling of Christ itself.

As program director of hunger education for ELCA World Hunger, Cumming is known to many throughout the church for his provocative writings on how people of faith might respond to situations of human suffering, including his articles and book on war and racism. In this volume he joins the other contributors in making clear the present challenge: discovering a new vision of structural injustice and the power that overcomes it.

It should be noted that ELCA World Hunger provided for the filming of all the symposium lectures. These video resources will be made available along with this book to congregations that are committed to the study of Luther's economic reforms and their meaning for today. Based on these lectures as well as filmed interviews with each of the presenters, Cumming has produced for this book a number of questions to guide discussion. We are grateful for your response.

CHAPTER ONE

Luther and the Common Chest

Carter Lindberg

The Reformation commemorations underway include many crucial topics related to Luther and the reform movement he unleashed. One topic missing, however, from the discussions is economics and social welfare,[1] a subject Luther hammered away at from the Ninety-five Theses (1517) to his late tract "Exhortation to the Clergy to Preach Against Usury" (1540). This omission reflects, in the felicitous phrase of Paul Wee, "the forgotten Luther," the Luther who initiated the reform of social welfare that eventually led to the welfare states of Germany and the Nordic countries.[2]

Now, how, you ask, can any aspect of a character like Luther, about whom more has been written than anyone else in church history, be forgotten? Already back in 2003, the German television channel ZDF ran a popular contest to identify the ten "best" Germans, and Luther came in second after the post-war chancellor, Konrad Adenauer. Can the "wisdom" of so many Germans be wrong? And lowly old Wittenberg, the boondock town Luther regarded as the very edge of civilization is now a UN designated world historical site, and, along with other Luther sites, a cash cow for tourism and Luther souvenirs. And lest there be any doubt that Luther is not forgotten, Playmobil recently issued tens of thousands of little Luthers! Produced for German tourism, the Luther figure is the fastest selling Playmobil of all time. This could be dangerous kitsch because, like the stately statues of Luther, he holds an open Bible; and someone might just read in it that the last shall be first, the mighty shall be put down, and the hungry fed. Indeed, a graphic motif in the Reformation was the "world turned upside down," the reversal of social estates.[3]

The Luther who throughout his life excoriated an unregulated profit economy and created social welfare programs is forgotten because he just does not fit an ideology that he said "dresses up greed." "How skillfully Sir Greed can dress up to look like a pious man if that seems to be what the occasion requires, while he is actually a double scoundrel and a liar."[4] "Greed is good" is not merely the mantra Gordon Gecko used to justify himself in the movie *Wall Street*,[5] it is an underlying ideology of our society. Greed received theoretical respectability by Adam Smith and practical application in "trickle down" economics. The latter policy, as John Kenneth Galbraith defined it, is that "If a horse eats enough oats, eventually there will be something in the road for the sparrow."[6] The conflict between the common good and self-seeking is not new of course. The same words and rationalizations were used in Luther's day: *Gemeinnutz* and *Eigennutz*"[7] We don't have space to review Luther's life-long attacks on the profit economy, other than to note that they are integral to his theology and social welfare programs. He realized that an "imitation of Christ" theology that idealized poverty as the ideal Christian state and viewed alms as the means to purchase paradise supported a profit economy that rationalized itself with charity. [8] If "almsgiving atones for sin" and "delivers from death" (Ecclesiasticus 3:30; Tobit 4:9-11; 12: 9), and "faith is formed by charity," there is no reason to address the systemic injustice of poverty. To be sure, the biblical mandate to feed the poor is non-controversial. What is controversial is why people are poor and hungry. Luther's relevance to our context is his analysis of poverty and his forceful advocacy of government policies to promote the common good. Luther's theological turn led him beyond remedial philanthropy to address the social and political roots of poverty. In this he foreshadowed the famous comment by the late Brazilian Archbishop Dom Helder Camara: "When I give food to the poor, they call me a saint. When I ask why the poor have no food, they call me a communist."[9]

Although some scholars have described Luther as the first political economist,[10] Luther understood himself as a pastor and theologian radicalized by his grasp of justification by grace alone. We are named in God's last will and testament, and since Christ, the testator, has died the will is in effect and we have inherited all that is Christ's.[11] Since salvation is received—not achieved—salvation is the foundation for life not its goal. Hence both poverty and almsgiving lose saving significance. Justification by grace alone undercut the explanatory function of the medieval ideology of poverty that fatalistically presented poverty and riches as the divine plan. The de-spiritualization of poverty enabled the recognition that poverty is a personal and social evil to be combated in terms of justice and equity. Luther thus asserted: "Poverty, I say, is not to be recommended, chosen, or taught; for there is always enough of that by itself, as He says (John 12:8): 'The poor you always have with you,' just as you will have all other evils. But constant care should be taken that, since these evils are always in evidence, they are always opposed."[12]

Faith active in love rooted in God's promise and testament is experienced in worship. The "sacrament is rightly called 'a fountain of love.'"[13] Playing on the word for worship, *Gottesdienst*, Luther states, "Now there is no greater service of God [*Dienst gottis*] than Christian love which helps and serves the needy, as Christ himself will judge and testify at the Last Day, Matthew 25[:31-46]."[14] For Luther social ethics flows from worship; it is the "liturgy after the liturgy." "That is how a Christian acts. He is conscious of nothing else than that the goods which are his are also given to his neighbor. He makes no distinction but helps everyone with body and life, goods and honor, as much as he can."[15] Faith active in love is indeed personal, but not privatistic. Worship and social welfare are inseparable.[16]

Under the rubric of Deuteronomy 15:4, "There will be no poor among you," Luther and his Wittenberg colleagues proceeded to establish social welfare programs.[17] "Luther was concerned to develop prophylactic as well as remedial social assistance. 'For so to help a man that he does not need to become a beggar is just as much of a good work and a virtue as to give alms to a man who has already become a beggar' (LW 13:54)."[18]

The first social welfare ordinance, the "Common Purse" (*Beutelordnung*), was passed by the Wittenberg Town Council with Luther's assistance in late 1520 or early 1521. "The charitable gifts were to be collected in church and distributed to the local poor. Where possible, a surplus of grain and wood should be collected for distribution in times of need. The new arrangement of charity appears to have begun to function in Wittenberg immediately."[19] The next major step influenced by Luther was the Wittenberg Order of January 1522. It is known as the "Common Chest" because a chest for the weekly collection and disbursement of funds was built with three separate locks and keys. Four stewards were elected on the basis of their knowledge of the town and the citizens' needs. The only criterion for distribution of loans or outright gifts was to be the need of the recipient. Initially funded by expropriated ecclesiastical endowments and then by taxes, gifts, and wills, the Wittenberg Order prohibited begging (directed at the Mendicant Orders and swindlers[20]); provided interest-free loans to artisans, who when established were to repay them if possible; provided for poor orphans, the children of poor people, and poor women in need of dowries for marriage; provided refinancing of high-interest loans at 4 percent annual interest for burdened citizens; supported the education or vocational training for poor children; and vocational retraining for under-employed artisans.[21] The Common Chest also soon added the services of the physician Melchior Fendt (1486-1564). Paid by the Common Chest, he worked as town physician on behalf of the poor. In addition to the expenses of the doctor and medications, the Common Chest paid for hot baths and bath cures for healing particular illnesses, along with hospitals for those with mental as well as physical maladies, and as such laid the foundation for modern social health care.[22] The Common Chest functioned as a kind of central bank for communal poor relief that was now a responsibility of the state. It was a new institutional creation that had not existed anywhere prior to the Reformation. Well-provided and staffed, the Common Chest order introduced a "professionalization of social welfare" that became widespread and continued into the early nineteenth century.[23] To the objection that social welfare was open to abuse, Luther replied, "He who has nothing to live should be aided. If he deceives us, what then? He must be aided again."[24]

The Wittenberg Common Chest quickly attracted the attention and emulation of cities with preachers influenced by Luther, including Augsburg, Nuremberg, and Altenburg in 1522, and Kitzingen, Strasbourg, Breslau, and Regensburg in 1523, as well as areas such as Hesse.[25] It also appeared in pamphlet propaganda such as "A Conversation Concerning the Common Chest of Schwabach" that urged readers "to read the booklet by Luther on the order of the common chest."[26] That booklet was Luther's preface to the Leisnig "Ordinance of a Common Chest."[27] After repeated requests for his assistance, Luther visited Leisnig (a small town southeast of Wittenberg) in September 1522 and was personally involved in the town's establishment of a Common Chest. Its elected ten directors included all classes—two from the nobility, two from the town council, three from the citizenry, and three from the rural peasantry. The chest itself was built with four different locks and kept in a secure place in the church; the keys were assigned to representatives of the different groups of directors. Three detailed record books were also maintained and kept in the chest along with funds. The directors met weekly and were to give triennial reports to the entire community. The initial capital funding was again from expropriated ecclesiastical revenues to be supplemented by taxes determined by the assembly, to be used "for no other purpose than the honor of God, the love of our fellow Christians, and hence for the common good."[28]

The further development and spread of Reformation social welfare through Common Chest ordinances was carried on by Luther's Wittenberg colleague and pastor, Johannes Bugenhagen (1485-1558).[29] In constant demand throughout northern Europe, Bugenhagen wrote or edited church orders for Braunschweig (1528),[30] Hamburg (1529), Lübeck (1531), Pomerania (1535), Denmark-Norway (1537), Schleswig-Holstein (1542), Braunschweig-Wolfenbüttel (1543), and Hildesheim (1544). He also influenced developments in south Germany through the work of the Strasbourg reformer, Martin Bucer. Known as the "Reformer of the North," Bugenhagen's contributions to social welfare legislation and its enactment were rooted in Luther's theology. "Faith active in love is the theological basis and practical motivation for the care of the poor in Bugenhagen's theology. He . . . maintains that caring for the poor is not a matter of free choice for the Christian but a clear expectation."[31] Bugenhagen contributed not only to the establishment of common chest orders but also improved them by separating funds for poor relief from funds for schools, pastors' salaries, and church maintenance. He pointed out that pastors can now boldly appeal for social welfare because people will know they are supported by salaries and thus not lining their own pockets.

The establishment of the Reformation through church ordinances which included provisions for social welfare and education was rooted in evangelical preaching and legally structured by jurists. Luther and his colleagues were fully aware that religion and politics are inseparable. Their social welfare programs required legal establishment as well as political support from princes and town councils.[32] "A whole coterie of sixteenth-century jurists and moralists built on Luther's core insights to construct intricate new Lutheran theories of law, politics, and society. Foremost among these were: (1) Philip Melanchthon . . . (2) Johannes Eisermann, a student of Melanchthon . . . and (3) Johann Oldendorp, Melanchthon's correspondent and Eisermann's colleague at the University of Marburg . . . . These three legal scholars, and scores of other German jurists and moralists who worked under their influence, brought many of Luther's cardinal theological teachings to direct and dramatic legal application."[33]

Eisermann, also known as Ferrarius, studied theology, medicine, and the classics at the University of Wittenberg before receiving his law degree there in 1532. He became a counselor to Landgrave Philip of Hesse and founding law professor of the new Lutheran University of Marburg. Eisermann is of particular interest through his development of "a Lutheran social contract theory" and his legal and political development of Luther's emphasis upon "the common good." Eisermann's tract "On the Common Good" (*Von dem gemeinen Nutz*, 1533) went through several editions, expansions, and translations including English. "Eisermann contemplated an active Christian magistrate at the core of an active Christian welfare state: '. . . to enlarge the common good, to relieve the poor, to defend the orphan and the widow, to promote virtue, to administer justice, to keep the law . . .'"[34]

As you know, Luther himself was no slouch at reminding the political authorities of these responsibilities.[35] Luther insisted that government is not only responsible for defending its people, it is also responsible for the nurture and education of its people.[36] The second virtue of a prince after securing justice "is to help the poor, the orphans, and the widows to justice and to further their cause."[37] In his explanation of the fourth petition of the Lord's Prayer in his Large Catechism, Luther wrote: "It would therefore be fitting if the coat of arms of every upright prince were emblazoned with a loaf of bread instead of a lion or a wreath of rue, or if a loaf of bread were stamped on coins, in order to remind both princes and subjects that it is through the princes' office that we enjoy protection and peace and that without them we could neither eat nor preserve the precious gift of bread."[38] In this advocacy, Luther did not limit himself to letters and tracts but spoke truth to power from the pulpit. The church orders themselves "are a kind of sermon."[39] Luther affirmed: "Christ has instructed us preachers not to withhold the truth from the lords but to exhort and chide them in their injustice. . . . [W]e must rebuke the Pilates in their error and self-confidence. Then they say to us, 'You are reviling the majesty of God,' to which we answer, 'We will suffer what you do to us, but to keep still and let it appear that you do right when you do wrong, that we cannot and will not do.' . . . For one should not remain silent about injustice nor let sin go unrebuked."[40]

For Luther a function of preaching is "to unmask hidden injustice, thus saving the souls of duped Christians and opening the eyes of the secular authorities for their mandate to establish civil justice."[41] Such "unmasking" of injustice, Luther asserted, is not done in a corner but in the preaching office "in the congregation," "openly and boldly before God and men." It is God's will, Luther continues, "that those who are in the office [of ministry] and are called to do so shall rebuke their gods [rulers] boldly and openly. . . . To rebuke rulers is not seditious, provided it is done in the way here described: namely, by the office by which God has committed that duty, and through God's Word, spoken publicly, boldly, and honestly. . . . [A] preacher is neither a courtier nor a hired hand. He is God's servant and slave . . . he is to do what is right and proper, not with a view to favor or disfavor, but according to law, that is according to God's Word, which knows no distinction or respect of persons."[42] Luther was equally blunt to his congregation saying he "was tired of preaching to them" and threatening to abandon the pulpit "if the people of Wittenberg did not contribute more generously to the common chest supporting pastors, students, and the poor."[43] Like his mentor, St. Paul, Luther was a master of "frank speech."

Commemorations tend to lionize the subject commemorated. In Luther's case this is an ever-present temptation for his heirs because Luther was really quite an astounding person and churchperson. In commemorating the 500th anniversary of the posting of the Ninety-five Theses, we have an ecumenical responsibility to remember and to advocate those aspects of Luther's work submerged by our culture's displacement of the common good by unjust social structures.

In closing we may recall Luther's letter to his friend and fellow Augustinian at Erfurt, John Lang. Written in May 1517, some five months before the Ninety-five Theses, Luther wrote: "Our theology and St. Augustine are progressing well, and with God's help rule at our University. Aristotle is gradually falling from his throne, and his final doom is only a matter of time. It is amazing how the lectures on the *Sentences* [scholastic theology] are disdained. Indeed, no one can expect to have any students if he does not want to teach this theology, that is lecture on the Bible or on St. Augustine or another teacher of ecclesiastical eminence."[44]

There are, I think, two points of interest here. First, Luther speaks of "our theology." He understands from the beginning that while his conversion experience was intensely personal, faith active in love is also communal. As we noted in relation to the common chest ordinances, innumerable pastors, lawyers, politicians, and laypeople were involved in developing the new social welfare legislation. From the beginning of the Reformation untold pastors and preachers labored to instill the elementary mandate to love our neighbor through addressing systemic issues of justice and welfare. Their emphasis along with Luther and Bugenhagen upon Matthew 25 held that such social concern is not only a consequence of proclamation but is a mark of the church.[45]

Second, Luther states that the reforming movement is rooted in curriculum reform! As one who has spent untold hours in faculty meetings discussing curriculum reform this sounds crazy, or at least counter-intuitive. But Luther's experience and his point here is that reform springs from the rock from which we were hewn. I know this sounds like special pleading since I've labored long as a church historian. Yet, look at seminary curricula. How much time is spent on "how" to pastor and how much time is spent on "why"? To what extent have the social sciences of psychology and sociology –the "Aristotles" of our time— displaced time for biblical studies, theology, and church history? How many seminaries have courses—even just one elective—on the history and theology of church care for the poor, on the history of diaconia? We lack a designated institutional resource for fostering research on the fundamental questions and praxis of diaconia such as the Institute for Diaconal Studies at the University of Heidelberg. As Paul Wee has stated: "The socioeconomic dimension of the Reformation has been conspicuously absent from the curricula of Lutheran seminaries and, consequently, from preaching and teaching in Lutheran congregations." "[T]his lost dimension of Reformation history and theology is urgently needed to inform the mission of the church today."[46]

Endnotes

1 Tom Scott, *Early Reformation in Germany: Between Secular Impact and Radical Vision* (Farnham, Surrey: Ashgate, 2013), 34n.1: "No recent scholarly German biography of Luther has made more than passing reference to his comments on contemporary social and economic issues." However, the Evangelical Church in Germany has included this topic, especially through its Sozialwissenschaftlichen Institut (ekd.de/si). See also the "Luther 2017–Kolumne at Deutscher Kulturrat" (kulturrat.de/text.php?rubrik+89; "Radicalizing Reformation" (reformation-radical.com/index.php/en/); and Philipp Koch, *Gerechtes Wirtschaften. Das Problem der Gerechtigkeit in der Wirtschaft im Lichte lutherischer Ethik* (Göttingen: V & R unipress, 2012). There are a few studies in English: Carter Lindberg, *Beyond Charity: Reformation Initiatives for the Poor* (Minneapolis:

Fortress Press, 1993); idem, "Luther on Wall Street and Welfare," *Logia. A Journal of Lutheran theology* 23/4, 2014: 7-12; Foster R. McCurley, ed., *Social Ministry in the Lutheran Tradition* (Minneapolis: Fortress Press, 2008); Samuel Torvend, *Luther and the Hungry Poor: Gathered Fragments* (Minneapolis: Fortress Press, 2008); Sean Doherty, *Theology and Economic Ethics: Martin Luther and Arthur Rich in Dialogue* (New York: Oxford University Press, 2014); Paul A. Wee, "Reclaiming Luther's Forgotten Economic Reforms for Today," *Lutheran Forum* 48/1, 2014: 52-56.

2   "[I]t is no coincidence that the first welfare states of the world originated in countries with Lutheran denominational background." "Protestant Ethics and the Modern Welfare State. Late Effects of the Reformation" Conference of the Evangelische Akademie zu Berlin, April 4-5, 2014 (eaberlin.de/nachlese/chronologisch-nach-jahren/2014/pr…). Albrecht Peters, *Kommentar zu Luthers Katechismen* Vol. 1: *Die Zehn Gebote* (Göttingen: Vandenhoeck & Ruprecht, 1990), 275: Luther's interpretation of the seventh commandment points in the direction of the welfare state. See also Sigrun Kahl, "The Religious Roots of Modern Poverty Policy: Catholic, Lutheran, and Reformed Protestant Traditions Compared," *Archives européens de sociologie* 46/1 (2005), 91-126 (also online); Gerhard Wegner, "Wer sorgt sich um die Armen? Der moderne Sozialstaat ist auch aus Luthers Geisterwachsen" and Heiner Lück, "Urahnen des Grundgesetzes?" in *EKD. Das Magazin zum Themenjahr 2014. Reformation und Politik: "Fürchtet Gott, ehret den König,* 10-11 & 18-21. [online]. The well known historian Karl Holl (1866-1926) had already made the point in 1911 that the Common Chest ordinances were the "first seed for the development of the social state." Karl Holl, *Gesammelte Aufsätze zur Kirchengeschichte I: Luther* (Tübingen: Mohr, 1948), 510; cf. Karl Holl, *The Cultural Significance of the Reformation*, tr. by Karl & Barbara Hertz and John Lichtblau (Cleveland: Meridian Books, 1959), 95. Antti Raunio notes: "A strong case can be made for Lutheranism's contribution to establishing a welfare state, but Lutheran theology and Lutheran churches often are ambivalent in their embrace of this kind of society." Raunio, "Luther's Social Theology in the Contemporary World" in Christine Helmer, ed., *The Global Luther: A Theologian for Modern Times* (Minneapolis: Fortress Press, 2009), 210-27, 213.

3   For these images see Carter Lindberg, *The European Reformations*, 2nd ed., (Oxford: Wiley-Blackwell, 2010), 154, 206. Luther's commentary on the Magnificat (1521; LW 21, 295-358) was written for the young prince, John Frederick, as a "Fürstenspiegel," i.e., instruction. The pre-Reformation spiritualization of poverty translated Mary's "low estate" in terms of humility instead of poverty. Matthew 5:3 does the same with the Luke 5:3 passage by shifting poverty from need to poverty of spirit. See Christoph Burger, *Tradition und Neubeginn. Martin Luther in seinen frühen Jahren* (Tübingen: Mohr Siebeck, 2014), 110-179: "Luther als Ausleger des Magnifikat."

4   "The Sermon on the Mount," 1532. LW 21, 183. See "Treatise on Good Works" (1520, LW 44, 107): "Greed has a very pretty and attractive cover for its shame; it is called provision for the body and the needs of nature. Under this cover greed insatiably amasses unlimited wealth."

5   See Phyllis A. Tickle, *Greed: The Seven Deadly Sins* (New York: Oxford University Press, 2004), 43, 81 n. 49. Centuries earlier, Bernard de Mandeville

(d. 1733) argued in his *Fable of the Bees* that private vice has public benefit. See also Ricardo Rieth, *"Habsucht" bei Martin Luther: Ökonomisches und theologisches Denken, Tradition und soziales Wirklichkeit im Zeitalter der Reformation* (Weimar: Böhlau, 1996).

6　Cited by Rich Klein in Galbraiths' obituary in *The Boston Globe*, May 1, 2006: A3.

7　In the sacrament, Luther wrote, self-seeking love ("eigennützigen Liebe") is driven out by the love that seeks the common good ("gemeinnützigen Liebe"). "The Blessed Sacrament of the Holy and True Body of Christ, and the Brotherhoods" (1519. LW 35, 45-73; here 67 = WA 2:754, 10-16). See Winfried Schulze, "Vom Gemeinnutz zum Eigennutz. Über den Normenwandel in der ständischen Gesellschaft der Frühen Neuzeit," *Historische Zeitschrift* 243 (1986): 592-626, 600: "Eigennutz" [selfishness, striving for personal gain] was the most frequently used term in the sixteenth-century anti-monopoly writings. The praise of "Eigennutz" and self-love for the benefit of others was already set forth in the 1564 tract by Leonhard Fronsberger, *Von dem Lob dess Eigen Nutzen*, well before the eighteenth-century works of Adam Smith and others.

8　See Berndt Hamm, "Den Himmel kaufen; Heilskommerzielle Perspektiven des 14. bis 16. Jahrhunderts" in Rudolf Sundrup & Jan R. Veenstra, eds., *Himmel auf Erden/Heaven on Earth* (Frankfurt: Lang, 2009), 23-56.

9　*Dom Helder Camara: Essential Writings* (Maryknoll, New York: Orbis Books, 2009).

10　Karl Marx was the first to do so. See his "Ökonomische Manuskripte und Schriften 1858-1861" in *Karl Marx/Friedrich Engels, Gesamtausgabe*, II. Abteilung, Bd. 2 (Berlin, 1980), 35. See Hermann Lehmann, "Luthers Platz in der Geschichte der politischen Ökonomie" in Günter Vogler, Siegfried Hoyer, Adolf Laube, eds., *Martin Luther. Leben-Werk-Wirkung* (Berlin: Akademie-Verlag, 1986), 279-94; 292f.: Luther held up before his contemporaries the devastating and disintegrating force of capital.

11　"A Treatise on the New Testament, That Is, the Holy Mass" (1520), LW 35, 88-89. See Berndt Hamm, "Martin Luther's Revolutionary Theology of Pure Gift without Reciprocation," *Lutheran Quarterly* 29/2 (2015): 125-161, here 138-9: "One can express the revolutionary radicality of Luther . . . quite succinctly. God's gift of salvation to human beings, like the gift of justification, is a pure gift without a gift in return." That is, God's gift has no strings attached.

12　"Lectures on Deuteronomy" (1525), LW 9, 148.

13　"The Babylonian Captivity of the Church" (1520), LW 36, 46.

14　"Ordinance of a Common Chest. Preface" (1523), LW 45, 172. Luther had already made this point in his "Short" and then "Long" sermons on usury (1519/1520): LW 45, 306-7; WA 6: 7-8; WA 6: 59,7-12, 24-29 where the term "Gottisdienst" is used for serving the neighbor. See also my *Beyond Charity*, 100-104, and Michael Beyer, "Theologische Grundlagen für Martin Luthers Sozialengagement" in Stefan Oehmig, ed., *Medizin und Sozialwesen in Mitteldeutschland zur Reformationszeit* (Leipzig: Evanelischen Verlagsanstalt, 2007), 53-72, especially 56, 62; and idem, "Wirtschaftsethik bei Martin Luther" in Udo Kern, ed., *Wirtschaft und Ethik in theologischer Perspektive* (Münster: Lit Vl., 2002), 85-110, 109.

15 "The Sacrament of the Body and Blood of Christ—Against the Fanatics" (1526), LW 36, 352-53.

16 See my *Beyond Charity*, and Torvend, *Luther and the Hungry Poor*, 127 with reference to Cynthia Moe-Lobeda, "Globalization in Light of Luther's Eucharistic Economic Ethics," *Dialog* 42/3 (2003): 252.

17 "Lectures on Deuteronomy" (1525), LW 9, 147-48; WA 14, 675, 22-24. Luther already advanced this text in his 1520 "To the Christian Nobility of the German Nation," LW 44, 189-90; WA 6, 450, 22-27; and in "Trade and Usury" (1524), LW 45, 281 (from the 1520 treatise on usury, WA 6, 41f.). See also my translation of the tract by Luther's colleague, Andreas Bodenstein von Karlstadt, "There Should Be No Beggars Among Christians," in C. Lindberg, ed., *Piety, Politics, and Ethics: Reformation Studies in Honor of George Wolfgang Forell* (Kirksville: Sixteenth Century Journal Publishers, 1984), 157-66.

18 Lindberg, *Beyond Charity*, 119. Reference to "Commentary on Psalm 82" (LW 13, 54).

19 Martin Brecht, *Martin Luther. His Road to Reformation, 1483-1521*, tr. by James Schaaf (Fortress, 1985), 374. See also Stefan Oehmig, "Über Arme, Armenfürsorge und Gemeine Kasten mitteldeutscher Städte der frühen Reformationszeit" in idem, *Medizin und Sozialwesen*, op.cit., 73-114.

20 See Luther's Preface to "On the Roguery of the False Beggars" (1528), LW 59, 236-239. Luther had already called for the abolition of begging in his 1520 appeal to the Christian nobility (LW 44, 115-217; 189-90: "One of the greatest necessities is the abolition of all begging. . . . Nobody ought to go begging among Christians. . . . Every city should support its own poor, . . . [rather than] the many vagabonds and evil rogues who call themselves mendicants." See Thomas Kaufmann, *An den christlichen Adel deutscher Nation von des christlichen Standes Besserung* (Kommentar zu Schriften Luthers, 3) (Tübingen: Mohr Siebeck, 2014), 384-91. It is in reference to such roguery that Luther affirms the saying of 2 Thess. 3:10 that he who does not work shall not eat.

21 A translation of Hans Lietzmann, ed., *Die Wittenberger und Leisniger Kastenordnung* (Berlin: de Gruyter, 1935) is in Lindberg, *Beyond Charity*, 200-202. See also "Die Ordnung des Rates der Stadt Wittenberg von 24. Jan. 1522" in Hans-Ulrich Delius, ed., *Martin Luther. Studienausgabe* (Berlin: Evangelische Verlagsanstalt, 1982), 525-29; and Theodor Strohm & Michael Klein, eds., *Die Entstehung einer sozialen Ordnung Europas*, vol. 2: *Europäische Ordnungen zur Reform des Armenpflege im 16. Jahrhundert* (Heidelberg: Winter, 2004), 12-19.

22 Stefan Oehmig, Ðer Wittenberg Gemeine Kasten in den ersten zweieinhalb Jahrzehnten seines Bestehens (1522/23 bis 1547) . . ." *Jahrbuch für Geschichte des Feudalismus* 12 (1989) & 13 (1989); here 13:141-45, 173. Fendt served on the medical faculty of Wittenberg University; his epitaph is in the city church. Robert Jütte, "Die Sorge für Kranke und Gebrechliche in den Almosen- und Kastenordnungen des 16. Jahrhunderts Anspruch und Wirklichkeit" in Oehmig, ed., *Medizin und Sozialwesen*, op.cit., 9-21, here 21.

23 Stefan Oehmig, "Über Arme und Bettler, Kranke und Waisen und ihre obrigkeitliche Handlung in Wittenberg in der Frühen Neuzeit" in *Wer nit arbeitet, soll auch nit essen . . .? Die neue Frage nach der Arbeit* (Wittenberger Sonntagsvorlesungen; Wittenberg: Drei Kastenien, 2007), 100-124; 116-19.

24 "Lectures on the First Epistle of St. John" (1527), LW 30, 278.

25 See for example, Gottfried Seebass, *Das reformatorische Werk des Andreas Osiander* (Nürnberg: Verein für Bayerische Kirchengeschichte, 1967), 181-83 re the influence of Wittenberg for the city's new poor ordinance. See also Anneliese Sprengler-Ruppenthal, *Zur Entstehungsgeschichte der Reformatorischen Kirchen- und Armenordnung im 16. Jahrhundert. Eine Dokumentation*, 83 pp. www.sprengler-ruppenthal.de/docs/zur_Entstehungsgeschichte.pdf. The collection of church orders begun by Emil Sehling is now approaching 24 volumes. Emil Sehling, ed., *Die evangelischen Kirchenordnungen* des VI. Jahrhunderts (Leipzig: Riesland, 1902-) now continued by the Heidelberg Akademie der Wissenschaften.

26 "A Conversation Concerning the Common Chest of Schwabach, Namely by Brother Heinrich, Knecht Ruprecht, Spitler, and Their Master of the Wool Trade" (1524) in Oskar Schade, ed., *Satiren und Pasquille aus der Reformationszeit*, vols. 1-3 (Hildesheim: Olms, 1966), 3:196-206. Partial translation by Lindberg in C. Lindberg, ed., *The European Reformations Sourcebook*, 2nd ed. (Oxford: Wiley-Blackwell, 2014), 78-79.

27 LW 45, 159-94. See also Strohm & Klein, op. cit., 20-41, and Karl Dummler, "Die Leisniger Kastenordnung von 1523," *Zeitschrift für evangelischer Kirchenrecht* 29/1-2 (1984), 337-53.

28 LW 45, 192; 189.

29 For Bugenhagen's contribution to social welfare see Tim Lorentzen, *Johannes Bugenhagen als Reformator der öffentlichen Fürsorge* (Tübingen: Mohr Siebeck, 2008), and idem, "Theologie und Ökonomie in Bugenhagens Fürsorgekonzept" in Irene Dingel & Stefan Rhein, eds., *Der späte Bugenhagen* (Leipzig: Evangelische Verlagsanstalt, 2011), 151-74. See also Kurt Hendel, "Johannes Bugenhagen, Organizer of the Lutheran Reformation," *Lutheran Quarterly* 18/1 (2004): 43-75; idem, "Paul and the Care of the Poor during the Sixteenth Century: A Case Study" in R. Ward Holder, ed., *A Companion to Paul in the Reformation* (Leiden: Brill, 2009), 541-71.

30 An English translation of the Braunschweig "Order of the Poor Chest" is in Kurt Hendel, ed. & tr., *Johannes Bugenhagen. Selected Writings*, 2 vols., (Minneapolis: Fortress Press, 2015), II: 1390-99.

31 Kurt Hendel, "The Care of the Poor: An Evangelical Perspective," *Currents in Theology and Mission* 15 (1988): 526-32; 527.

32 Unfortunately, the legal aspects of Reformation social welfare have not been extensively researched. For a recent literature review see Hannes Ludyga, *Obrigkeitliche Armenfürsorge im deutschen Reich vom Beginn der Frühen Neuzeit bis zum Ende des Dreissigjährigen Krieges (1495-1648)* (Berlin: Dunckeer & Humblot, 2010), 16-26. The substantive studies by the American John Witte, Jr. are not mentioned. See John Witte, Jr., *Law and Protestantism. The Legal Teachings of the Lutheran Reformation* (Cambridge: Cambridge University Press, 2002).

33 Witte, *Law and Protestantism*, 9.

34 John Witte, Jr., "An Evangelical Commonwealth: Johannes Eisermann on Law and the Common Good" in David Whitford, ed., *Caritas et Reformatio: Essays on Church and Society in Honor of Carter Lindberg* (St. Louis: Concordia

Publishing House, 2002), 73-87, 83. See also sections on Eisermann in Witte, *Law and Protestantism.*

35 See "Treatise on Good Works" (1520). LW 44, 50: "Here [re injustice] we must strive against spiritual and temporal authorities . . ." See Eike Wolgast, *Die Wittenberger Theologie und die Politik der evangelischen Stände* (Gütersloh: Mohn, 1977), 287: Instruction and exhortation of the authorities was an important factor of the public activity of the clergy.

36 Gisela Kahl, "Martin Luther, 'der älteste deutsche Nationalökonom',' *Wissenschaftliche Zeitschrift* 33/3 (1984), 315-326, 317; Tom Scott, op.cit., 42-43; Philipp Koch, *Gerechtes Wirtschaften. Das Problem der Gerechtigkeit in der Wirtschaft im Lichte lutherischer Ethik* (Göttingen: V & R Unipress, 2012), 225.

37 "Commentary on Psalm 82" (1530), LW 13, 53. This commentary is another example of Luther instructing rulers by a "Fürstenspiegel." Much of this commentary focuses on justice and law serving the poor.

38 Robert Kolb & Timothy J. Wengert, eds., *The Book of Concord* (Minneapolis: Fortress Press, 2000), 450. See Albrecht Peters, *Kommentar zu Luthers Katechismen*, Band 3: *Das Vaterunser* (Göttingen: Vandenhoeck & Ruprecht, 1992), 128-130.

39 Annaliese Sprengler-Ruppenthal, "Fundierung der Kirchenordnungen," online www.sprengler-ruppenthal.de/page1002.html.

40 WA 28, 360-61; LW 69, 236-37; see LW 44, 51.

41 Heiko A. Oberman, "Teufelsdreck: Eschatology and Scatology in the 'Old' Luther" in idem, *The Impact of the Reformation* (Grand Rapids, Michigan: Wm. B. Eerdmans Publishing Co., 1994), 62.

42 "Commentary on Psalm 82," LW 13, 49-51. In his sermon on Matthew 5 (1530/1532), Luther stated: "For Christ has not instituted and appointed the preaching office so that it serves for gaining money, goods, favor, honor, and friendship or thereby to seek advantage, but rather that [through it] the truth is freely and openly proclaimed to reprove evil and to proclaim what is necessary for the good, salvation and blessedness of the soul." WA 32, 304, 21-24.

43 Editor's introduction to "Sermon on the Gospel of St. John. Chapters 17-20" LW 69, 135. See WA 27, 409-411; WA 32, 4, 16f.; WA Br 5, 222, #1521. See also Brecht, op.cit., 2: 289; 3: 258-65.

44 LW 48, 42.

45 See Friedrich Löblein, *Prediger der Barmherzigkeit im 16. Jahrhundert*, 2 vols. (Heidelberg: Winter, 2013).

46 Paul A. Wee, "Reclaiming Luther's Forgotten Economic Reforms." 52, 55.

CHAPTER TWO

"Greed Is an Unbelieving Scoundrel"

Samuel Torvend

The point is, ladies and gentleman, that greed is good. Greed is right. Greed works. Greed clarifies, cuts through, and captures the essence of the evolutionary spirit. Greed in all of its forms—for life, for money, for love, for knowledge— has marked the upward surge of mankind. And greed— mark my word—will not only save this one company but that other malfunctioning corporation, the USA.[1]

Laudato si'

On June 18, 2015, the second encyclical of Pope Francis was officially published and released in eight languages. The title of the encyclical, *Laudato si'*, was drawn from the first words of the canticle written by Francis of Assisi in the early thirteenth century.[2] In English, the encyclical's title reads: *Praise Be to You: On Care for Our Common Home.* On the one hand, his Holiness draws on the work of contemporary scientists who warn of global warming. He points out the dark side of free market capitalism and its offspring, rampant consumerism. He laments irresponsible development and degradation of the environment. He offers a cogent link between the unfettered accumulation of wealth sanctioned by capitalism, the degradation of the earth and its many species, and the growing plight of those who are impoverished throughout the world. A *deconstructive* motif runs through the encyclical. On the other hand, the Holy Father presents a sacramental vision of the earth as God's living, growing, and interrelated gift in which every creature holds significance. He speaks of the intimate relationship between economic, environmental, and social ecology: an "integral ecology" in which economic and social systems can be reformed to support and sustain the earth and all its inhabitants, not simply the wealthy earth-plundering few who reside in

North America, Western Europe, and East Asia.[3] There is a *reconstructive* motif running through the treatise.

"I hope I'm not going to get castigated for saying this," said Jeb Bush, candidate for the presidency. "But I don't get economic policy from my bishops or my cardinals or my pope. . . . I think religion ought to be about making us better as people and less about things that end up getting in the political realm."[4] One wonders if Mr. Bush, a Roman Catholic, was unaware of the many statements on economic life and ecological care published by the United States Conference of Catholic Bishops—not only statements but countless letters written by laypersons, bishops, religious, and priests to Congress and the White House. [5] Yet Mr. Bush is not alone in his apparently limited awareness of those ecclesial statements on the economy and the environment "that end up getting in the political realm."

In a 2012 survey of 100 Lutheran clergy, seven were aware that Luther had written "something" about the creation and something about the economy ("Was it about loans?" wondered one clergyperson), but only three had actually read any of these works and had done so while students at seminary. "Are you aware that the ELCA has published statements on economic life and on the environment?"[6] While eighty were aware of the documents, only eight had read them.[7] Between these two—a layperson's resistance to ecclesial statements and clergy ignorance of them—the church finds itself today.

Is it possible that cultural values at odds with the Gospel of Jesus Christ are so powerful that those listening to their preachers and teachers ("my bishops and my pope") are responsive only to those ecclesial messages that seem to confirm such cultural values? Or this: Have church leaders been so thoroughly trained in the "consolation" of the Gospel of Jesus Christ that they have become deaf to the prophetic stream that courses through the Scriptures, the Christian tradition, and their own theological legacy? Indeed, what is lost when laypeople, bishops, theologians, and clergy have little or no idea that they possess a vital tradition of engagement with economic, social, and political issues?[8]

Lutheran Passivity

The confession upon which the church stands or falls, wrote Luther, is the teaching on justification by grace: a justification and a grace received in utter and *absolute passivity*. Indeed, the writings of the reformer and the subsequent outpouring of Lutheran theology and preaching have emphasized a posture of receptivity, of *inactivity*, as a constituent element in this theology of grace.[9] At the same time, Luther insisted on the careful discernment between Law and Gospel in preaching and teaching: the preacher leading listeners to despair of their ability to keep the Law and thus turning in grateful relief to the promise of forgiveness in the Gospel. In this mode of preaching, personal failure meets a highly personalized word of absolution and promise "for *you*." And yet one wonders if such an overwhelming stress on the posture of passivity and forgiveness as the preeminent gift of the Gospel engenders a highly individualistic caste to faith and a passive posture toward the world.

Or say it this way: Does the Lutheran insistence on maintaining an absolute and clear distinction between "two kingdoms"—Christ ruling in one, civil authorities in the other—actually nurture distance from the "kingdom of this world"? Is it possible that well-intentioned Christians might "engage the world" or "serve the neighbor" by responding with charity to pressing need and yet find it difficult to discern why their charitable activity is needed in the first place? If there is no knowledge of the critical tradition of Christian engagement with economic, political, or social conditions—*conditions which might actually produce the very suffering to which charity responds*—is theological leadership not diminished or, worse yet, rendered impotent in its mission to enlighten and guide?

Oh, yes, one can readily assert, "Baptism is for living and living in this world," yet ignore the very conditions, systems, and cultural values that contribute to if not create human and ecological suffering. Charitable initiatives, the bread and butter of Christian service in the world, can actually temper the possibility of raising critical questions and provoking critical action on behalf of justice.

Theological Anthropology

Luther's intense promotion of passivity in the presence of justifying grace complemented his theological anthropology. At odds with the late medieval teaching that all humans are fundamentally good though seriously flawed by sin, Luther claimed that humans are profoundly turned inward such that the individual recognizes only the self as the primary subject in the world. Such curvature ("crookedness," he called it) makes it impossible for humans to be in "right" relationship with their Creator and their neighbors. For the Reformer, this spiritual curvature ends only at death and yet the therapy of the Gospel serves as a potent antidote, drawing the Christian to grow in trust of God and love for the neighbor. Thus Luther argued for what he considered a realistic view of human nature, one in which the Christian should never be surprised by human fault—nor despair of the power of grace.[10]

For the Reformer, only God can break into the inward curve of human life with an act of liberation—a shock to the "normality" of congenital narcissism—and begin the life-long process of creating "right" relationship with others. While "alien righteousness" makes progress throughout life and is perfected at death, it is the animating source of social or worldly righteousness "that follows the example of Christ . . . who did all things for us . . . and so desires that we also should set the same example for our neighbors."[11] In effect, Luther's dialectical propensities gave birth to a spirituality marked by tension and struggle: between the innate tendency to focus on the self alone and the possibility of living in this world with and for others.

Avarice in Christian Thought

Yet such "worldly living" never exists apart from the economic, social, and political fabric of life. And it was in this "fabric" where Luther's teaching on greed and its economic effects emerged, allowing the biblical witness to interrogate the conditions which can produce injustice, suffering, and violence. Of course, Luther was not the first theologian to write about avarice or greed. Indeed, his teaching rests within the larger stream of Christian tradition focused on social ethics. Consider Evagrius Ponticus (345-399), the desert monk, who included greed in his list of deadly sins to be named and combated: deadly to the soul whenever the Christian failed to trust God and God's providential care of God's children.[12] Given his erudition and persuasive style of writing, Evagrius' writing on greed was translated from Greek into Latin becoming influential in Western European Christianity. Indeed, Gregory of Rome (540-604), oft-quoted by Luther, revised Evagrius' list of deadly sins, placing greed in third position after lust and gluttony, and chiding his clergy who, prior to Gregory's reform of church life, seemed especially susceptible to avarice.[13]

In the high Middle Ages, Thomas Aquinas (1225-1274) linked inordinate love of self with the desire for more and more. "Every sinful act," he wrote, "proceeds from the inordinate desire for some temporal good. The fact that anyone desires a temporal good inordinately is due to the fact that he loves himself inordinately."[14] Such inordinate love, claimed Aquinas, leads to contempt for God. In the same century, Dante Alighieri (1265-1321), quoting the New Testament in its condemnation of avarice as "the root of all evils" (1 Timothy 6:10), spoke of greed as the sinful inclination most opposed to love. It was, he said with a degree of autobiographical bitterness, the source of political corruption in society.[15] While he was forgiving of lust and gluttony, Dante considered greed a capital crime against one neighbor's due to its addictive power and senseless regard for the good of others.[16]

Luther's Sensitivity to Greed

Luther's sensitivity to *avaritia,* to avarice, is first heard in the twenty-eighth of his Ninety-five Theses where he notes, "It is certain that when money clinks in the money chest, greed and avarice can be increased."[17] The desire for more and more is a power within the soul that grows outward, a subtle and crafty force capable of cloaking itself in new forms that appear pleasing, even godly, to the eye but are in fact deadly: "Why does not the pope," he asks, "whose wealth is today greater than the wealth of the richest Crassus [the "wealthy fat one"], build this one basilica of St. Peter with his own money rather than with the money of poor believers?"[18] While Luther was fond of excoriating church leaders and institutions for the ways in which they accrue wealth under the guise of a "godly" work, he was quick to condemn business persons who did the same. Consider this example he draws from his observation of trading practices in Wittenberg:

> A merchant from a distance comes to me and asks me if I have such and such goods for sale. Although I don't have them I say "Yes" and sell them to him for ten or eleven gulden. I buy the goods [to sell him] cheaper than I am selling them to him. . . . Thus I deal with his money and property without risk, trouble, or labor, and I get rich.[19]

"The merchants have a common rule," he writes, "which is their chief maxim: 'I may sell my goods as *dear* as I can.'[20] They think this is their right. Thus occasion is given for avarice, and every window and door to hell is opened. What else does it mean but this: I care nothing for my neighbor."[21] Stealing motivated by greed is so widespread that people pay little attention to it.[22] Thus Luther linked greed with the commandment that forbids theft, for in it "God has commanded us all not to rob or pilfer our neighbor's possessions."[23] Set next to the command is what Luther witnessed in his own town of Wittenberg: businesspersons cheating their neighbors with defective merchandise, false measures, and taking advantage of their customers "through deception and crafty dealings." In utter exasperation he wrote: "This is the most common craft and largest guild on earth!"[24]

Is stealing the same as greed? The scholastic theologians offered a clear distinction between the two. Indeed, medieval canon law actually protected the starving person or parent with hungry children who stole but stole foodstuffs or crops in order to stay alive. Luther recognized greed as more deadly than theft, without diminishing the wrong committed against one's neighbor in "stealing or pilfering his or her possessions." Indeed, he would have recognized the sculpted image of greed on the column in many Gothic churches: a man with mouth opened wide, bent over, and holding two large bags of coins, one in each hand. Luther prayed that Christians would be delivered from the "gaping jaws of avarice," an insatiable appetite—a mouth perpetually opened, waiting to consume more—a hunger within the soul that is never satisfied.[25]

Greed knows no limit; it possesses an addictive property that grasps for more money, more possessions, more personal status, and more property. And yet it only deepens one's crookedness or inward curvature. "As long as I have my profit and satisfy my greed, of what concern is it to me if it injures my neighbor in ten ways at once?"[26] This is the strange working of greed: The object of its desire can be gained and gained repeatedly, yet it produces only deeper alienation from other human beings, objectifying and then abusing them.

Luther had little difficulty in bringing to light the power of greed in business dealings: "These [thieves] sit in their chairs and are known as honorable, upstanding citizens while they rob and steal under the cloak of legality."[27] Yet his ire was also directed at political leaders. "We might well keep quiet here about individual petty thieves since we ought to be attacking the great powerful archthieves *with whom lords and princes consort and* who daily plunder not just a city or two, but all of Germany."[28] The princes are charged by God to ensure justice and equity as guardians of the law and as protectors of the people: "It is their duty to use their duly constituted authority in punishing the injustices of the merchants and preventing them from so shamefully skinning their subjects."[29]

And yet: "I hear that [the princes] have a finger in [collusion with monopolies], and thus the saying of Isaiah [1:23] is fulfilled, 'Your princes have become companions of thieves.' They hang thieves who have stolen [little] but do business with those who rob the whole world and still more than all the rest."[30] Political leaders are susceptible to bribery from powerful interest groups: indeed, the trading monopolies "line the pockets of princes and magistrates with gold and silver." They enjoy the company of flatterers. With all others, they are prone to serve their own avaricious interests, placing personal gain above care for the common home—the *oeconomicus*—of the state.[31]

As Ricardo Rieth points out, "Luther did not consider any social or professional class greedier than the others. He intended, instead, to identify and condemn greed in functions fulfilled by all members of all classes (*Stände*)."[32] It comes as no surprise, then, that in his commentaries on the seventh commandment, Luther speaks of the many who are plagued by greed: day laborers, workers, servants, artisans, burgers, butchers, shoemakers, farmers, tailors, beer makers, owners of trading monopolies, church leaders, magistrates, and princes. All persons live within the tension between the inward curve where avarice grows and the power of grace to turn one in generosity toward the neighbor in need. Price manipulation, price fixing, charging exorbitant interest rates, appropriation of land for personal or corporate rather than civic and public use, accepting bribes to thwart the regulation of abusive business practices, the ever-present yearning for more and more with no sense of limitation or sufficiency, the eager desire for some measure of social mobility—all these practices and aspirations wreak havoc in the "common home" and mock care for the common good. The worst effects of greed can be curbed through government regulation of the banking industry, the investigation of price-fixing and prosecution of the law, outlawing abusive loan practices, and citizen protest against misappropriation of land.[33] But Luther knew this as well from his own life and what he witnessed in his own city: the heart turns slowly to the Word of God and its power to transform greed into liberality.

A Profound Form of Sin

With the medieval theologians, Luther understood greed as a profound form of sin, a dry wind that evaporated love for the neighbor. At the same time, his teaching on greed was cast in terms of idolatry, the devout worship of increasing material gain, this worship in conflict with worship of the living God, the author of all life, health, and salvation. Or one might say it this way: The failure to trust and thus worship God is a form of unbelief. Where God is not trusted, where God is not worshipped, other gods emerge and ask for one's trust, one's loyalty. It is these other gods who will order all other relationships and concerns in one's life. Thus, it is possible to read the Scriptures, participate in the reformed Mass, listen to the preacher, receive the Lord's Body and Blood, tithe, sing beautiful hymns, and yet live a "lawless" and "pagan" life because one is, in reality, captive to the pernicious yet subtle desire for more and then more.

> There are some who think that they have God and everything they need when they have money and prosperity; they trust in them so stubbornly that they care for no one else. They, too, have a god, mammon by name . . . on which they set their whole heart. . . . This desire for wealth clings and sticks to our nature all the way to the grave.[34]

Idolatry

For Luther, greed is a form of idolatry, of failing to believe in God (*unglaube*). It is also the source of injustice (*ungerechtigkeit*) in society: the one who trusts and worships the little god of the self and the self's desire for more and more, will pay scant attention to the commands of God which counsel Christians to "help and support one's neighbors in all of life's needs . . . love and honor one's spouse . . . improve and protect the property of one's neighbors . . . defend and speak well of one's neighbors ... help and serve the neighbor in keeping what is theirs."[35] For Luther, Christian faith—trust in God—enlightens *every* aspect of life, animates loving service to the neighbor, and prompts public resistance to injustice whether that injustice is discerned in banking, law, politics, or trade, in the local store or the multinational corporation.

Luther knew well that personal and institutional greed thwarted care for society's most vulnerable members: "The poor are defrauded every day, and new burdens and higher prices are imposed."[36] While he argued that political leadership should lead in helping "the poor, the orphans, and the widows to justice and to further their cause,"[37] he also recognized that growing income disparity in a profit economy produced social anxiety and a growing underclass of impoverished persons, many of them children. Consequently, his enthusiastic approval of the church order developed in Leisnig, a town that had accepted "the pure Gospel," was one significant instance in which theological reform and civic practice joined in a project of "structured generosity" for the homeless, the hungry, those impoverished by economic crises or natural disasters, persons unemployed or chronically sick, widows and widowers with no family support, orphans, and indigent strangers.[38]

The Leisnig Project

In his preface to the "Fraternal Agreement on the Common Chest of the Entire Assembly at Leisnig,"[39] he wrote, "Greed is a disobedient and unbelieving scoundrel" that, nonetheless, can be quenched by "Christian love that helps and serves the needy."[40] While he despaired of anyone heeding his economic reforms—"I fear that very few will be guided by my advice"[41]—he brought considerable energy to this project that would be imitated throughout Germany and the Nordic countries and, in time, become what North Americans and Western Europeans know as state-funded social assistance. Luther was not an expert in public policy; his reforms were guided by the Scriptures as they shed light on and interrogated his economic and social milieu. [42] "The holy gospel, now that it has come to light, rebukes and reveals all the 'works of darkness,' as St. Paul calls them in Romans 13 [:12]. For it is a brilliant light, which illumines the whole world and teaches how evil are the works of the world and shows the true works we ought to do for God and our neighbor."[43]

The Leisnig project was guided by the Joseph, "a teacher of the promises of God," who oversaw the creation and management of a regional food supply in preparation for drought and famine (Genesis 41). The disaster relief director in ancient Egypt shed light on Luther's Germany: "It becomes [the duty of] the princes to provide for the poor, and especially those who are in their earliest years, lest they perish from hunger."[44] The Leisnig initiative was inspired by the example of the apostles "who set up a common fund" for those in need (Acts 2:44-45; 4:32-35); the Corinthian Christians who contributed to a common collection, a form of disaster relief (2 Corinthians 9); and the counsel of Christ who will "judge and testify at the Last Day" (Matthew 25:31-46). Luther and his friends in Leisnig had every hope that "structured generosity" might quench the power of greed through a communal commitment to assist the most vulnerable and easily abused in their society. Acutely aware of the conditions that can produce human suffering, this "evangelical" experiment was created as counterpoint to and criticism of political lassitude and corporate greed.

"A Brilliant Light"

With his university colleagues and pastoral collaborators, Luther shared in the humanist call to "return to the sources" of classical antiquity as a way to restart and reform their lives and the life of their society at the birth of what we call early modernity. The calamities of the late Middle Ages, the complexity of theological discourse and church law, and the corruption of business, governmental, and religious leaders prompted a profound yearning for change that, at the beginning of their century, seemed impossible. For the Wittenberg reformers, the ancient sources were the Scriptures, freshly translated into the vernacular, the writings of the early Christian bishops and teachers, and record of Christian practice in its earliest centuries.

In our culture, one that lives in the present moment alone, it can be a challenge to grasp how a return to the past could in any way "restart" the present and immediate future. Yet that reforming project was not so much a return to the past, an act of nostalgia for a "golden age," but a willingness to let the ancient text serve as a "brilliant light, which illumines . . . [the] evil works of the world and shows the works we ought to do for God and our neighbor."

One wonders if the little known economic writings and projects of the university professor who came to be called the *Propheta Germania*, the prophet of Germany, might serve as light—perhaps not a brilliant light, but a light nonetheless—that illuminates the prophetic tradition of economic justice infrequently claimed by his spiritual daughters and sons. What did he say? "I am content if only one or two follow me, or would at least like to follow me. I have done what I can. God help us all to do what is right and to stand firm."[45]

Endnotes

1 Oliver Stone and Stanley Weiser, *Wall Street* film (Los Angeles: Twentieth Century Fox, 1987).

2 The text is commonly found in hymnals with the title "All creatures of our God and King," a poor translation of the original.

3 For the text of Laudatio si', see The Holy See, "Encyclical Letter Laudatio si' of the Holy Father Francis on care for our common home" online at http://w2vatican.

va/content/franceso/encyclicals/documents/papa-francesco_20150524_enciclica-laudato-si.html (accessed December 4, 2015).

4 Carol Davenport, "Pope's Views on Climate Change Add Pressure to Catholic Candidates," the *New York Times,* June 16, 2015. Online at http://www.nytimes.com/2015/06/17/us/politics/popes-views-press-gop-on-climate-change:html (accessed December 4, 2015).

5 To mention only a few of the documents published by the United States Conference of Bishops, see U.S. Conference of Bishops, "A Place at the Table," Nov. 13, 2002; "Global Climate Change: A Plea for Dialogue, Prudence, and the Common Good," June 15, 2001; "A Jubilee Call for Debt Forgiveness," April 1999; "A Catholic Framework for Economic Life," 1996; "Renewing the Earth," Nov. 14, 1991; and "Economic Justice for All," 1986; all online at http://www.usccb.org (accessed December 4, 2015).

6 See ELCA "Economic Life: Sufficient, Sustainable Livelihood for All" online at http://www.elca.org/Faith/Faith-and-Society/Social-Statements/Economic-Life and "Caring for Creation: Vision, Hope, and Justice" online at http://elca.org/Faith/Faith-and-Society/Social-Statements/Caring-for-Creation (both accessed December 4, 2015).

7 The survey was conducted at an ELCA Northwest Washington Synod study conference held in Everett, Washington.

8 Luther's writings that treat of economic and related political questions include but are not limited to his Lecture on Psalm 82, Lecture on Amos, sermons on The Sermon on the Mount, Treatise on the Blessed Sacrament of the Holy and True Body and Blood of Christ and the Brotherhoods, Disputation on the Power and Efficacy of Indulgences, The Address to the Christian Nobility of the German Nation Concerning the Reform of the Christian Estate, The Large Catechism, Sermons on the Ten Commandments, Treatise on Good Works, Trade and Usury, Ordinance of a Common Chest, Preface: Fraternal Agreement on the Common Chest of the Entire Assembly at Leisnig, Admonition to the Clergy That They Preach Against Usury.

9 Consider Luther's "A Brief Instruction on What to Look for and Expect in the Gospels" (LW 35:117-124); "Sermon on Two Kinds of Righteousness" (LW 31:297-306); and "The Freedom of a Christian" (LW 31:333-377).

10 I am mindful of the sermon preached by the pastor of St. Francis Lutheran Church (San Francisco) on Sunday, August 23, 1998, after former president Bill Clinton made a public confession of his affair with White House intern Monica Lewinsky. The preacher noted that the editors of the *New York Times* were incredulous after Clinton's confession. "How could a president of such great stature and with so much to lose betray his spouse and his supporters and cause damage to the highest political office in the land?" The preacher paused and then, in my recollection, said: "To anyone familiar with Luther's understanding of the human condition, this comes as no surprise whatsoever, for none of us—president or pastor or postal worker—is immune from making utterly stupid and grievous mistakes."

11 "Two Kinds of Righteousness" (LW 31:300).

12 Richard Neuhauser, *The Early History of Greed: The Sin of Avarice in Early Medieval Thought and Literature* (Cambridge: Cambridge University Press, 2006), 47-57.

13 See Letter 1.38 in *The Letters of Gregory the Great:Books 10-14*. Vol. 3, with introduction, translation, and notes by John R. C. Martyn (Toronto: Pontifical Institute of Medieval Studies, 2004), 784-785.

14 See Thomas Aquinas, *Summa Theologica,* Ia-IIae, q. 77, art. 4, online at http://www.sacred-texts.com/chr/aquinas/summa/sum214.htm (accessed December 4, 2015).

15 Banned from his beloved Florence, Dante never lost sight of the political leaders in the Black Guelph party who opposed his affiliation with the White Guelphs in the battle for control of the city.

16 Dante treats of avarice in the *Inferno*, Canto VII. See *Inferno* at the Princeton Dante Project, online at http://etcweb.princetonedu/dante/pdp/ (accessed December 4, 2015).

17 "Disputation on the Power and Efficacy of Indulgences" (LW 31:28).

18 Ibid. (LW 31:33). Let us note that Julius II (1503-1513) envisioned the new St. Peter's as the site for his own magnificent tomb, designed but never completed by Michelangelo Buonarroti, an ambitious plan not lost on Luther.

19 "Trade and Usury" (LW 45:265).

20 That is, "at the highest price possible."

21 "Trade and Usury" (LW 45:247).

22 See "The Large Catechism" (BC 416).

23 Ibid.

24 BC 417.

25 BC 245-246.

26 "Trade and Usury" (LW 45:247).

27 Ibid.

28 In the critical edition of BC, the editors note that "the words in italics [see above] were included in the first two editions of the Large Catechism printed in Wittenberg and Erfurt in 1529. However, they were already removed while the first Wittenberg edition was in the press, probably by the printer. The passage was restored in the German *Book of Concord* (1580)," BC 417. One wonders: was pressure placed on the printer to remove this reference to the very persons who were considered the political guardians of the emerging reform movement? Would offense be given?

29 "Trade and Usury" (LW 45:270).

30 Ibid.

31 From Greek oikos: household; oikonomia: household management. Latin: oeconomia.

32 Ricardo Rieth, "Luther on Greed" in *Harvesting Martin Luther's Reflections on Theology, Ethics, and the Church*, ed., Timothy Wengert (Grand Rapids: Wm. B.

Eerdmans Publishing Co., 2004), 166. See also Rieth's larger work, *"Habsucht" bei Martin Luther. Ökonomisches und theologisches Denken. Tradition und Wirklichkeit im Zeitalter der Reformation* (Weimar: Böhlau, 1996).

33 The first section regarding trade in "Trade and Usury" (LW 45:245-273).

34 "The Large Catechism," BC 387.

35 "The Small Catechism," BC 352-353.

36 "The Large Catechism," BC 418.

37 "Psalm 82" (LW 13:53).

38 See my *Luther and the Hungry Poor: Gathered Fragments* (Minneapolis: Fortress Press, 2008).

39 LW 45:169-176.

40 Ibid., 170, 172.

41 "Ordinance of a Common Chest" (LW 45:170).

42 See Peter Matheson's masterful discussion of the eruption of biblical images in the sixteenth century and the economic, political, and social effects of these powerful images in his *The Imaginative World of the Reformation* (Minneapolis: Fortress Press, 2002).

43 "Trade and Usury" (LW 45:245).

44 "Lectures on Genesis" (LW 7:159).

45 "Ordinance of a Common Chest" (LW 45:176).

CHAPTER THREE

The Subversive Luther

Cynthia Moe-Lobeda

I begin with a word of thanks to Paul Wee, Conrad Braaten, and the other organizers for their vision and long hard work in creating this symposium. I am honored to be here with a number of people from whom I have learned so much. Carter Lindberg's *Beyond Charity* was central to my understanding of Luther's economic ethics; I thank Carter for that extraordinary work. And Phil Anderson has for decades modeled a dedication to justice for so many of us.

Let us dig in. How many of you were aware of the WTO protests in Seattle in 1999? During those protests I was reading Luther and his economic ethics. I was stunned to hear that his words denouncing the emerging capitalism of his day (although of course it did not yet go by the name of capitalism) were almost identical to the protesters' words! "Well," I thought, "maybe I am just imagining this congruence." So I tested it during a talk I was giving at Augustana College. I read words from Luther and from the protesters and asked people to vote on which was which. They could not tell the difference!

Luther—like the protestors—called people to defy the emerging capitalism of his day because it hurt the poor whom Christians are called to love. His world-shaking claims about justification were radical resistance to social systems that sucked people away from remembering who they were as recipients of God's love and as beings who lived that love into the world.

I was bewildered! "How could it be," I have pondered ever since, "that a tradition sprung from such roots could have remained largely (though not entirely) complicit with contemporary capitalism and other power arrangements that suck us away from living as if we are indeed beloved creatures of God *who live God's love into the world by resisting what damages vulnerable neighbors?* What on Earth has happened to tame this splendidly powerful heritage?"

This is the question we explore in this hour. But we explore it for the sake of an even more important question. How could Lutheranism and Lutheran understandings of justification be *re-reformed* to claim our heritage of resistance?

In response to these questions, we will look into four of Luther's subversive discoveries regarding justification. Each has two faces. I will argue that North Atlantic Lutheranism has tended to embrace only the safe face of these earth-shaking claims—the face that does not disrupt the reigning power alignments of our contexts but rather reinforces them.

Then we will note the life-giving power to be found in re-embracing the subversive face of these four claims. It is the power to be found in drinking from the wellsprings of our radical heritage in order to build ways of life that first trust the gracious love of God and then embody it in the world it by living toward economic justice for all.

Luther's Subversive Claims

First subversive claim: Two kinds of righteousness

Luther rattled the world with his radical claim that God, rather than human works, make us righteous. God gives, he explains, two kinds of righteousness. The first places us in an utterly different relationship *with God*; we are totally forgiven and become righteous in God's sight.

As a "fruit and consequence" of this first gift, we are placed in a radically different relationship *with people* by the "second kind of righteousness." It, he writes, is a manner of life spent in "good works" that serve the wellbeing of the neighbor.

Luther's understanding of justification is, thus, transformative. Justified sinners gradually are changed by the righteousness of Christ into people who seek the well-being of others. The startling implications for economic life will become evident shortly.

Luther's notion of justification as transformation does not contradict the centrality of sin in his theology. Luther understands sin as self turned in upon self, the human proclivity to do everything for the promotion of self, out of concern for self, and using resources claimed as one's own rather than as gifts of God. Luther argues that humans cannot free themselves from this condition. Only God can do so as an undeserved gift. God can grasp and turn the sinner. I will argue shortly that, in Luther's theology, it is the power of the indwelling Christ and Spirit that "turns" sinners, empowering us gradually, although never perfectly, to love with the actual love of Christ within.

One of Luther's important contributions is his insistence that justification as transformation is not justification as moral perfection. Christians remain simultaneously sinners and righteous. They are "rusty tools, being polished by God for as long as they live."

Luther's understanding of what happens to people when they are made righteous by God coheres with his central convictions that works do not and cannot *cause* salvation. They *follow from* salvation.

But unlike later Lutheranism, Luther also insisted that works are a vital part of life for people who are justified by Christ. "Faith," he writes, "is followed by works as a body is followed by its shadow." And elsewhere: "Faith in Christ does not free us from works but from false opinions concerning works, that is, from the foolish presumption that justification is acquired by works."

The form of "works" relevant here are the works that embody "love to our neighbor." Luther preaches: "God makes love to our neighbor an obligation equal to love to himself." He identifies "two principles of Christian doctrine." The first principle is that Christ gave himself that we may be saved, and we are saved by no effort of our own. The second "is love . . . as he gives himself for us . . . so we too are to give ourselves with might and main for our neighbor." Luther insists on the inseparability of the two: they are "inscribed together as on a tablet which is always before our eyes and which we use daily."

That is, God gives forgiveness as gift, regardless of how broken we may be, and then sends us forth to be God's hands and feet while remaining faulty and imperfect in doing so. We become God's *"rusty tools"* (italics mine), Christ for the other through love for our neighbor. According to Luther, our shortcomings in fulfilling this calling are vast. Vaster yet is God's unfailing forgiveness of them.

Second subversive claim: Neighbor love as guide for economic life

For Luther, that norm of neighbor-love pertains to every aspect of life for the Christian, including economic life. According to him, economic activity is intrinsically an act in relationship to neighbor, and all relations with neighbor are normed by one thing: The Christian is to serve the neighbor's well-being, while also meeting the needs of self and household. Economic practices that undermine the wellbeing of the neighbor (especially of the vulnerable) are to be rejected and replaced with alternatives. About this Luther was vehement and specific.

Luther's German economic context included the gradual shift from an agricultural society to early modern capitalism. Consequences included high prices, growing disparity of wealth, and increasing poverty, especially of those with low or fixed income. The poor were increasingly a cheap labor pool for an expanding profit economy. Poverty was a growing social problem. Increasing "large"-scale international trade required capital which sought profitable investment. Thus, the ethics of capital transactions were in public discussion.

In this context, Luther helped to establish a local social welfare system that provided material goods and created jobs. He theologically denounced certain aspects of the emerging capitalist economy that exploited the poor—including the freedom of capital from political constraints—and admonished preachers to do the same. Hear Luther in his comments on the seventh commandment in the Large Catechism: Speaking of the "free public market," he writes, "Daily the poor are defrauded. New burdens and high prices are imposed. Everyone misuses the market in his own willful, conceited, arrogant way, as if it were his right and privilege to sell his goods as dearly as he pleases without a word of criticism."

Luther taught that widely accepted economic practices that undermined the well-being of the poor ought to be eschewed and replaced with alternatives. As alternatives, Luther established norms for everyday economic life that prioritized meeting human needs over maximizing profit as the aim of economic life. To illustrate: Christians, according to Luther, must refuse to charge what the market will bear when selling products if so doing jeopardizes the well-being of impoverished people. Christians may not buy essential commodities when price is low and sell when it is high, for so doing endangers the poor. Economic activity, he argued, should be subject to political constraints. "Selling ought not be an act that is entirely within your own power and discretion, without law or limit." Civil authorities ought to establish "rules and regulations," including "ceilings" on prices, he insisted.

Finally, Luther admonishes pastors regarding their roles and obligations in the face of economic practices that exploit the vulnerable.

Pastors are to "unmask hidden injustice." Luther goes so far as to admonish clergy to preach (for Luther, that is to speak the living Christ) against usury and to withhold the sacrament from a usurer unless he repents, for he is "damned like a thief, robber, and murderer."

In short, according to Luther, neighbor-love, as the norm for public life, has at least three dimensions:

- love manifest in service to neighbor, even if it brings danger to self and family;

- love manifest in disclosing and theologically denouncing oppression or exploitation of those who are vulnerable; and

- love manifest in ways of living that counter prevailing economic practices where they exploit the vulnerable or defy God in some other way.

Loving in these forms, we embody Luther's "second principle of Christian doctrine" (". . . to give ourselves with might and main for our neighbor").

Third subversive claim: Christ lives within and among us

These startling moves in economic life presuppose that believers will exercise the moral wherewithal to reject economic practices that imperil the vulnerable neighbor. This means rejecting the opportunity to maximize profit at the expense of the poor, for harming neighbor in this way would transgress neighbor-love. For Luther, this moral power was not a humanly generated virtue. Rather it comes to us as the presence of Christ dwelling within and gradually transforming the community of believers. Christians as objects of Christ's love become subjects of that love. The indwelling Christ, mediated by practices of the Christian community, transforms the faithful toward a manner of life that actively loves neighbor.

Luther nuances this role of Christ differently in various writings. There is not time here to go into that detail or to cite the sermons and treatises. Hear just one example:

> "[T]his is . . . one of the exceedingly great promises granted to us poor miserable sinners, that we should be . . . so highly honored as not only to be loved by God through Jesus Christ . . . but should even have the Lord Himself dwelling completely in us."

For Luther, this presence of Christ within believers and the believing community is the active love of Christ for the world working within human beings. This indwelling presence enables Christians to disclose and theologically denounce economic ways that exploit impoverished people and to generate alternative ways of living.

Resistance to dominant powers requires courage. According to Luther, the indwelling Christ and Spirit supply it. "The Hebrew word for spirit," Luther preaches, "might well be rendered 'bold, undaunted courage.'" We are made, he argues, "far more powerful through the Holy Spirit, and are undaunted by the world, the devil, death, and all kinds of misfortune." This empowering courage is, according to Luther, greater and more powerful than any other force on Earth. This courage empowers the risky moves entailed in neighbor-love where it transgresses exploitative economic norms and practices.

Fourth subversive claim: Obey and disobey ruling authorities

Luther's understanding of what was injustice was severely limited by a number of contextual factors including: 1) his anti-Semitic, Constantinian, and patriarchal worldview; 2) the nonexistence, in the pre-modern conceptual world, of the concept of organized social structural change; and 3) his conflating the orders of society with the orders of creation and with God's will. These factors, among others, led Luther to assume a divinely ordained social hierarchy, align himself with the political powers that enforced it, and admonish obedience to civil authorities as obedience to God. According to this norm of obedience, Luther considered rebellion against civil authority to be evil, more evil than murder, for rebellion against civil authority, he concluded, attacks the divinely established head and interferes with the divinely ordained function of rulers. Rebellion against civil authority could be, in Luther's estimation, demonic. Thus, in some arenas, Luther was aligned with terrible injustice which he did not perceive to be injustice and that he supported theologically. This is seen most clearly in his demonizing of Jewish people, and his denunciation of the peasant uprising and of the "radical" reformers.

Notable therefore is Luther's astonishing exception to this norm of obedience. He firmly admonished *disobedience to* temporal authorities when they demand ways of life that betray allegiance to God—including God's call to embody neighbor-love. As a public theologian uncritically committed to and theologically justifying the norm of obedience to civil authority, Luther demanded one exception to that norm. Where obedience to civil authorities contradicted obedience to God or to conscience in line with God, or where the demand of civil authorities ''tends toward the suppression of the Christian faith, the denying of the divine word," Christians, he taught, were "to resist them at least with words," and to "obey God . . . rather than men." In his "Letter to Frederick," Luther argues that human authority is not always to be obeyed, namely when it undertakes something against the commandments of God; yet it should never be despised but always honored.

According to Luther in 1523, that resistance could take the form of words and of refusal to hold certain beliefs. Yet by 1531, in "Dr. Martin Luther's Warning to His Dear German People," the mandate to resist became stronger. This "warning" contains one of Luther's strongest statements that where rulers disobey God or call Christians to disobey God, the rulers are to be resisted. "Whoever does obey him [the emperor] can be certain that he is disobedient to God and will lose both body and soul eternally in the war." Resistance, he said, could take even armed form because civil authorities were jeopardizing the proclamation of the Gospel and demanding that people disobey God. Where rebellion against civil authorities was for any other reason, it was wrong. In essence, where Luther finds the proclamation, hearing, and remembering of the Gospel to be at stake on a large scale, he calls for resistance to civil authorities.

What happens then when we hold together these four claims?

Held together, they entice us to remember who we are as both objects of God's love and agents of it, and they empower people for living according to God's love. That is, these claims *provide both the reason and the moral-spiritual power to defy political, economic, and cultural authorities and norms where they demand us to ignore, distrust, or contradict God's gift of right relationship with God and with neighbor.* This includes economic practices, policies, and systems that demand people to harm the vulnerable in order to maximize profit for self. To illustrate: The second kind of righteousness—with neighbor-love at its heart—would not allow Christians to profit at the expense of impoverished people. We could not, for example, condone inadequate wages in the quest of higher corporate gains. We could not buy products made cheaply by companies' failure to provide a living wage and health care benefits, and we could not condone public policy that allowed such moves. Neighbor-love would demand Christians to speak out against extractive industries that destroy communities in Ecuador, India, the U.S., and around the world in order to benefit shareholders.

This is not strange given that Luther himself vehemently denounced aspects of the emerging capitalist economy that he considered harmful to economically vulnerable people. The moral-spiritual power and "bold undaunted courage" for such transgressive and evangelical moves are—according to Luther—given to us by the power of Christ and Spirit dwelling within the believing community.

Embracing the Safe Side . . . Obscuring the Word

The subversive nature of these four faith claims, however, disappears if only the first and non-disruptive part of each is adopted. *Lutheran traditions in the ensuing 500 years have swerved toward adopting only the parts of each claim that did NOT disrupt but rather tended to reinforce reigning power arrangements and their ideological underpinnings. This includes the context of advanced global capitalism.* Consider again each of Luther's four subversive claims.

Two Kinds of Righteousness

Lutheran traditions have eagerly adopted the "first kind of righteousness" as the core of the Gospel. We are indeed made right with God by God's grace. God loves, fully accepts, and saves us despite our short fallings—however terrible they may be—and does this freely. Nothing that we do can change this saving reality. Centralizing this truth claim is one of Lutheranism's great contributions to humankind. It has meant life to me; I stake my life on this claim. To minimize it would be to betray Luther and the Gospel itself.

Yet, to uphold this first form of righteousness without upholding the second also betrays both Luther and the Gospel. While Luther insisted that two kinds of righteousness were inseparable, we have allowed the second to slip away. We have welcomed being made right with God without seeing that we are also to make right with neighbor, set on a course of living justly with neighbor that shapes all facets of life, both public and private.

While the first kind of righteousness threatened the life-shaping power structures of Luther's day, the second kind would threaten the power structures of ours, including the reigning form of an advanced global market economy. The second kind of righteousness could not tolerate growth at all costs and profit maximization for the wealthy despite its consequences for the impoverished.

Neighbor Love as Guide for Economic Life

Lutherans have been admirable in adopting the call to love neighbors in need by giving generously through such efforts as providing schools, health care, welfare relief, refugee resettlement, housing for homeless people, food for hungry people, and more. This good and faithful aspect of the Lutheran heritage represents the first of Luther's three forms of loving in economic life. The other two, however, North Atlantic Lutheranism, has tended to ignore.

It is far more risky to love by "disclosing and theologically denouncing oppression or exploitation," and by transgressing "prevailing economic norms that exploit the vulnerable." These forms of love would call into question nearly every economic move we make (buying, selling, investing). Loving in these ways would invite us to align our lives with the rapidly expanding global movement to create more socially equitable and ecologically sustainable economic principles, policies, and practices.

Christ as Indwelling Presence

Accepting Christ as means of forgiveness is a profound gift that Lutheranism has offered to the broader church and the world. Our weakness lies where we have ignored or minimized Christ also as indwelling presence. Accepting the eucharist and baptism as means of grace in which God offers forgiveness, we have not tended to preach and teach eucharist and baptism also as means of Christ's infinite power of love actually coming to abide within us.

Not naming and claiming this gift of Christ's indwelling presence, we are "off the hook" from taking seriously what it means for how we live in relationship to political, economic, military, and cultural systems that may exploit or even kill neighbors. If we take seriously that the God of justice-making love—who, in the form of a Palestinian Jew, defied the norms of the Roman Empire—lives within us, then are we not compelled to counter the norms of oppressive economic empire? Trusting the presence of Christ truly within us means trusting that infinite love, unstoppable even by torture and death, is a part of our very being. Standing up against exploitation of vulnerable neighbors becomes an act of Christic love breathing within us.

Obey and Disobey Ruling Authorities

Lutherans—at least in Euro and Euro-American traditions—have tended to uphold Luther's admonishment to obey secular authorities.

We have not however, given equal weight to his astonishing exception to that norm. It is the call to *disobey* temporal authorities when they demand ways of life that betray allegiance to God—including God's call to embody neighbor-love—or that obscure the proclamation, hearing, and remembering of the Gospel. Economic policies and practices that enable some to flourish at the cost of degrading or destroying countless others in our backyards and across the globe betray allegiance to the God of justice-making love. And they block our proclamation that God loves all and is working and willing toward abundant life for all.

Held Together

These moves to embrace the safe side of Luther's claims while ignoring the risky side open the door to a privatized understanding of justification. Freedom, then, is from inner demons produced by efforts to justify oneself according to the meritocracies of our day, but not freedom from systems of oppression that cost countless people their lives, livelihoods, or communities. Justification, then, changes my relationship with God but has little to do with how I relate to neighbors through economic, political, or military systems.

Choosing the safe side of Luther's claims enables us to live a privatized form of Gospel, escaping from its implications for the public or political side of life. This safe choice enables us to see the Gospel as freedom from private sin and despair but not as freedom from systemic sin. These moves detach Luther's world-shaking claims about justification from their political and economic consequences.

Luther was convinced that the greatest abuse of the church in his day was that "God's word has been silenced." People were prevented from hearing the Word and, through it, remembering who they were as recipients of God's love and as agents of it. Luther's liberating faith claims uncovered and refuted the belief systems and power structures responsible for obscuring God's Word and thus corroding trust in God.

By adopting only the safe side of his theological truths, we too obscure God's liberating Word about who we are as recipients and agents of God's love. We, thereby, truncate the power and meaning of justification. When "safety" and "risk" are held together, they are tremendously hope-filled assertions.

In Closing: Great Hope

They are hope-filled because they mean that Lutherans are blessed with an incredible gift. It is the invitation to re-affirm our closely held beliefs and open ourselves to the vast and life-giving potential that they hold. We may, in communities of faith, prayerfully and daringly risk living into the Gospel's power in public life. This is a terrain that Jesus walked at great cost and in which Luther was a daring and faithful traveler.

With Luther, we may venture boldly into long-ignored aspects of his claims, aspects that disrupt the power alignments and ideological gods of our day. If we trust God's love by holding firmly to the second kind of righteousness as well as the first, welcoming neighbor-love's call to renounce systemic injustice and build life-giving alternatives, embracing the power of Christic love abiding in us, and disobeying power structures that demand us to transgress the call to love neighbor as self, then we can more truly be "God's hands and feet on Earth." We will more faithfully honor Luther's daring, risky, evangelical discoveries about what it means to be justified by God's grace. And we will be a force to challenge systemic injustice and build more socially just and ecologically sustainable alternatives. In these ways, we trust God's gracious and transformative Word and embody it in the world. "The Word of God," Luther said, "wherever it comes, comes to change and renew the world."

In these faithful ventures and modes of living the Gospel we will be fallible, faulty, at times fearful, and encumbered by the incessant lure of self curved in on self—as was Luther and as (he vociferously assures us) are all human beings. However, that we are "rusty" tools makes us no less precious tools in God's sight and in God's liberating work on Earth.

Addendum: A Word about Theological Method

Two methodological assumptions inform this work. First is my understanding that theological inquiry as a critical constructive discipline entails three elements. They are: 1) critique of where the tradition has betrayed the Gospel or served the causes of death, destruction, or domination; 2) retrieval of suppressed or ignored elements of the tradition that are capable of igniting the fire of the Gospel in our day; and 3) reconstruction for the sake of being faithful to God. These elements may be sequential or they may be interwoven. Here, they are threaded together throughout.

Secondly, this chapter is grounded in an assumption regarding theological work in the Lutheran heritage. Lutheran inquiry into justification often focuses on asking what the message of justification by grace through faith means in each new time and place. I presuppose that inquiry into justification also should ask how dominant understandings of justification have undermined the proclamation and hearing of the Gospel, including its radical political-economic-cultural-ecological implications, and then should build on what is learned through that crucial critical query.

CHAPTER FOUR

An Economic Reading of Martin Luther's Catechisms in Long Context

Jon Pahl

I'm going to begin with three stories that I will, in due course, connect to my main point, which is that Martin Luther's Catechisms, both in what they critique and in what they encourage, promoted across very different contexts economic behaviors, anticipate what Nobel Laureate Muhammad Yunus first called "social businesses," or what have been dubbed, more broadly, "social enterprises."

In June 2009, while visiting Sweden for a conference on the history of children and youth, I decided to go to church. Because I was staying near Stockholm's Arlanda airport and because my colleague, Gordon Lathrop, had recommended that I visit the village of Sigtuna, I set out in my rental car on a rainy Sunday morning for St. Mary's Church. From what I understood of the church-going habits of Swedes, I expected the sanctuary to be nearly empty. But as I drove into the picturesque village that sits alongside Lake Mälaren, I was surprised to see a procession of young people in white robes walking along the street, carrying umbrellas. It was Confirmation Sunday—one of the few moments in life when a typical Swede, and their parents, would actually show up at church. The ancient edifice of St. Mary's Church—built in the thirteenth century, was packed.

On May, 21, 1972, I was confirmed at Faith Lutheran Church in Appleton, Wisconsin. Prior to my confirmation, I had experienced what has been, until quite recently, a fairly typical and rigorous process of catechesis: I spent two years in two-hour classes each Wednesday night, and an hour on Sunday morning, devoted to a study of Martin Luther's

Small Catechism. My study included memorizing the Catechism—and regurgitating it verbatim in both written and spoken form. But our study also included discussing how we might apply the teachings of the Catechism in daily life and to society—including to questions of social justice and economic life.

My third story evokes the quite recent past. On October 13, 2015, in the Democratic Party Debate in Las Vegas, Senator Bernie Sanders of Vermont, in a response to a question by Anderson Cooper about whether he was a capitalist, said, and I quote: "We should look to countries like Denmark, like Sweden and Norway, and learn from what they have accomplished for their working people." And in reply, Hillary Clinton said: "We are not Denmark. I love Denmark. We are the United States of America, and it's our job to rein in the excesses of capitalism so it doesn't run amok."

My brief talk today is to sketch out for further discussion the history of what we might call the forgotten Lutherans. In other words, I want to invite us to consider how Luther's most influential economic insights—his Catechisms, as interpreted through the centuries in the lives of millions of ordinary Lutherans, can explain why both Sanders and Clinton are correct. Beyond both state-sponsored solutions to poverty ("Denmark, Sweden, and Norway"—and we ought to add Germany to Sanders' list) and market-based solutions to poverty ("We are the United States of America. . . .") resides a third way of social enterprise. Social enterprises might just integrate what those Swedish youth and this American youth learned through the study of the Catechisms—that we are saved by grace, through faith—all of life is a gift and trust. And because our salvation is not a matter for anxiety, we are then free to engage rational practices and to organize strategically in ways that *incorporate* economic policies that benefit and protect vulnerable populations, and we are free to *incorporate* the kind of business practices that are both sustainable and produce discernible public benefit. Both of these kinds of collective economic action—whether by states or private citizens, I am willing to argue can find their historical origins, and their long evolution, in the Catechisms of Martin Luther. My talk has three sections. Section One is entitled "Context: Saved by Sacrifice or *The Better Angels of our Nature*?" Section Two is "An Economic Reading of the Catechisms." And a brief Section Three is entitled "A Third Way and Global Cultural Change Awaiting our Persuasive Advocacy and Participation."

Context: Saved by Sacrifice or *The Better Angels of our Nature*?

As a historian I am sinning boldly. That is, I am reading history backwards. All historians do it; I'm being honest about it. And my starting point is this: In "Denmark, Sweden, and Norway" (to use Bernie Sanders' shorthand) Lutherans (by and large) have created relatively equitable societies with strong supports for vulnerable populations. In the United States, Lutherans have created an impressive social service and advocacy network—the 300-plus agencies of Lutheran Services in America—during an era when inequality has risen dramatically and empathy for vulnerable populations often appears to have withered. So my historically heretical question—how did Lutherans turn out to be so darned above average? And my hypothesis is simply that the answer must reside, directly or indirectly, in by far the most influential of Martin Luther's publications—the Catechisms.

That economic inequality has grown since 1980 in America is inarguable. As Barbara Ehrenreich's many books document, along with films like Robert Reich's 2014 documentary *Inequality for All*, the numbers are clear across statistical measures. Real wages have stagnated for workers since 1979, while the percentage of income and wealth in the hands of the 1 percent has skyrocketed. I won't bore you with the numbers which can be accessed in many and various places. But while inequality in America has spun off imitators in the "greed is good" global sweepstakes—notably places like Turkey, Israel, and Greece, among other even less admirable plutocracies—in fact, around the globe poverty has declined. As the New York Times reported, drawing upon a UN Millennium Development Goals report released in July, in 1990 fully 47 percent of the world's population lived in "extreme poverty." In 2015 the number of people living on less than a $1.25 per day—which is the definition of "extreme poverty," was 14 percent. This is not to dismiss the very real suffering that endures around the globe; it is to point out, empirically, that human enterprise can make a difference in alleviating that suffering.

It also highlights how when it comes to economic inequality America is truly exceptional—as a refuge for greedy oligarchs. The problem, as I see it, is theological: what I called in my last book American "innocent domination." Innocent domination is when ordinary American citizens support with no ill malice policies that sacrifice their own interests for some supposedly noble and righteous cause or another. Those causes of "sacrifice" have shifted over the years—from anti-Communism to anti-

Islamism to anti-LGBTism to anti-Black Lives Matter and others. But over the past four decades, roughly, people in the U.S. have voted for representatives and leaders who do not do us justice. Whether this is "innocent" or not is a proposition I am willing to debate. But the problem, again, is theological: We (those of us who participate in political processes and who realize the potential of collective organizing and the need to craft rational policies) have been persuaded that our salvation (which is often reduced to economic terms under the sway of what David Loy has called the "religion of the market") depends upon one form of sacrifice or another; that is one kind of a substitution or scapegoat or construction of an enemy whose destruction will secure (supposedly) our own well-being. And an earlier version of that perversion of Christianity is what prompted Martin Luther's dramatic attempts to reform the church in the sixteenth century, as S. Mark Heim's helpful book, *Saved from Sacrifice*, puts it. And, as others on our panel have made quite clear, the economic lines from that Reformation to today can be sketched in fascinating and largely forgotten pathways, both in Northern European Lutheran state-led initiatives and in the history of voluntarist Lutheran social ministry organizations here in the U.S.

Now, it is common for Lutheran clergy with whom I occasionally converse to bemoan the "secularization" of Lutheran social ministry organizations in America. But, in fact, that secularization (we might also call it "professionalization" or "expertise") is of a piece with the long history that Harvard neuropsychiatrist Steven Pinker traced in his recent book, The Better Angels of our Nature: Why Violence has Declined. Pinker's big book, which enraged activists of many stripes, follows Immanuel Kant's 1893 "Essay on Perpetual Peace" to see three factors behind what he documents quite clearly is a dramatic decline over the past centuries in murder and inter-state warfare, and a dramatic increase in creature comfort, in empathy, and in the possibility of human flourishing (for instance, reductions in infant mortality and childhood morbidity). The three factors that Kant predicted and Pinker documented are democratic participation, trade, and international organization. Societies where people have a voice in political processes, and where violence is contained in legitimating structures, are more peaceful than those where they do not. The people of countries who trade with each other are less likely to kill each other than people whose countries do not engage in trade (murder being notoriously bad for business). And, finally, countries that participate in international cooperatives like the United Nations are more peaceful than those that do not. What Pinker fails to recognize, in typical cultured despising of the actual working of the world's religious traditions, is that far and away the most empathy-inspiring, durable, trade-engaged, and cooperative agencies that humans have created are our religions. Collectively, the social, material, and spiritual capital of religious traditions dwarfs the GNP of even the world's largest national economy, namely the U.S. at roughly $17 trillion. And over the past century, as Diana Eck and other historians of ecumenism and interfaith engagement have demonstrated, roughly from Mahatma Gandhi through Fethullah Gülen to Leymah Gbowee, the capacity of our traditions to engage empathy in cooperative endeavors on behalf of greater justice and peace has begun to bear real fruit. Lutherans have advanced two trajectories in this history of religiously-inspired engagement on behalf of greater justice and peace—in Northern European state-sponsored welfare programs and in American voluntary social ministries. And to understand what brings these two trajectories together in social enterprise requires an economic reading of Luther's Catechisms.

An Economic Reading of the Catechisms

Economics is implicit throughout Luther's Catechisms. As is well known, Luther shifted catechetical instruction to put the Ten Commandments first, and then the Creed—so as properly to differentiate Law and Gospel. All sections of both Small and Large Catechisms include an "a" and a "b"—Law and Gospel. The Law always accuses, mandating prohibitions and injunctions that we fail to observe. The Gospel saves, and then leads to specific behaviors/practices—not to save us, but to protect ourselves and others. And if we look at the patterns of Law and Gospel in the Catechisms, we can draw out economic implications that mandate and recommend specific economic behaviors that have been learned by Lutherans over the centuries (more or less) and applied in different contexts in very different ways. To see these implications we can read the Catechisms straight through, concentrating on the Small Catechism (since it was the most widely used), and engaging the Large Catechism to amplify what Luther intended or what the significance of the teaching in the Small Catechism might have been.

So, in Luther's preface to the Small Catechism he reports seeing in his own context "wretched deprivation" as a visitor to many German congregations (BC 347). By this phrase "wretched deprivation" Luther does not mean only that congregants lacked theological sophistication. Luther typically uses strong language that evokes economic as well as theological squalor: The people lived "like simple cattle or irrational pigs" (BC 347-8). In contrast, Luther offered his Catechism (and other initiatives) to encourage humanizing practices. He did so through persuasion, and what we might call today "capacity-building." "No one can or should force another person to believe" (BC 349). The first concrete example of what Luther intended is economic. He recommended that leaders in the church should teach the Catechisms, study them, and "put the greatest stress on that commandment or part where your people experience the greatest need. For example, you must strongly emphasize the Seventh Commandment, dealing with stealing, to artisans and shopkeepers and even to farmers and household workers, because rampant among such people are all kinds of dishonesty and thievery" (BC 349). The preface to Luther's Small Catechism thus sets an economic tone for the entire work: a) the prohibition of violent economic behavior, and then b) engagement in persuasion to build empathy and human capacity. Three times in the preface alone Luther writes against compulsion; these are matters we must work out together, as the entire form of the document suggests.

The first section of both Catechisms, then, is devoted to the Ten Commandments. As is well known among Lutherans, Luther's simple interpretation of the first commandment is: "You are to have no other gods. What is this? We are to fear, love, and trust God above all things." This does not appear, immediately, to suggest an economic reading. Yet it does suggest clearly that economics is penultimate. Contrary to much thinking then and now, the first commandment prohibits what we might call "economic reductionism," or imagining that any activity can be reduced merely to a calculation of profit and loss. That this economic reading of the first commandment is consistent with Luther's intent becomes clear in the Large Catechism, where he writes:

> So that it may be understood and remembered, I must explain this a little more plainly by citing some everyday examples of the opposite [of fearing, loving, and trusting God above all things]. There are some who think that they have God and everything they need when they have money and property; they trust in them and boast in them so stubbornly and securely that they care for no one else. They, too, have a god—mammon by name, that is, money

and property—on which they set their whole heart. This is the most common idol on earth (BC 387).

In short, in Luther's Catechisms, critique of *economic* idolatry is the first and most crucial point. He amplifies this emphasis with typically colorful invective. The idolaters Luther has in mind are "rich potbellies" and defiant "blockheads." But his intent is ultimately pastoral—to build empathy. "When people have devoted all their care and effort to scraping together possessions and great wealth, what have they accomplished in the end? You will find that they have wasted their effort and toil. Even if they piled up great riches, these have turned to dust and blown away. They themselves never found happiness in their wealth, nor did it ever last to the third generation" (BC 391). As Columbia economist Josef Stiglitz put it in his recent book *The Price of Inequality*—excess hurts even those who imagine that they benefit from greed. Greed is a delusion; an idol that harms all.

In Luther's treatment of the second commandment a similar economic implication becomes clear. "You are not to misuse the name of your God," the commandment reads. Luther's commentary goes on: "What is this? Answer: We are to fear and love God, so that we do not curse, swear, practice magic, lie, or deceive using God's name, but instead use that very name in every time of need to call on, pray to, praise, and give thanks to God" (BC 352). Note Luther's typically two-step discourse. Christianity, he asserts, first prohibits lying and other forms of speculative behavior ("magic"); then he invites and encourages instead the most honest use of language—gratitude and invocation of support—we are to "call on, pray to, praise, and give thanks to God." Luther would never interpret such language narrowly. In the Large Catechism, this economic reading of Luther's intent gains clarity. He writes: "Misuse of the divine name occurs first of all in business affairs and in matters involving money [and] property" (BC 393). After all, gratitude and trust is the foundation of every contract, cooperative effort, and policy: unless language is secure, nothing truly human happens.

When Luther turns to the fifth commandment, his interpretation similarly implies an economic reading. He writes: "You are not to kill. What is this? Answer: We are to fear and love God, so that we neither endanger nor harm the lives of our neighbors, but instead help and support them in all of life's needs" (BC 352). That this "support" includes economics is made clear in the Large Catechism, where Luther clarifies that not to kill means to do no harm in any aspect of bodily life: "God wants to have everyone defended, delivered, and protected from the wickedness and violence of others, and he has placed this commandment as a wall, fortress, and refuge around our neighbors, so that no one may do them bodily harm or injury" (BC 411). On the flip side, the commandment not to kill, Luther asserts, "is violated not only when we do evil, but also when we have the opportunity to do good to our neighbors and to prevent, protect, and save them from suffering bodily harm or injury, but fail to do so" (BC 412). Luther's examples are economic: "If you send a naked person away when you could clothe him, you have let him freeze to death. If you see anyone who is suffering from hunger and do not feed her, you have let her starve" (BC 412).

Not surprisingly, the way Luther interprets the seventh commandment is obviously rich with economic implications: "You are not to steal. What is this? Answer: We are to fear and love God, so that we neither take our neighbors money or property nor acquire them by using shoddy merchandise or crooked deals, but instead help them to improve and protect their property and income" (BC 353). Again, note the a-b, Law-Gospel structure. In the Large Catechism, Luther makes clear that he means to address systemic as well as individual economic matters. "Thievery is the most common craft and the largest guild on earth . . . Armchair bandits . . . rob and steal under the cloak of legality" (BC 417). We could go on, but I hope it is evident by now that Luther's interpretation of the commandments created what Lindberg (following Wuthnow) identified as "discursive fields." First—fear God, don't lie, don't kill, don't steal. Second—love God, help and support each other, help each other to protect and to improve property and income.

So, at least negatively—in what they prohibit, it would seem clear that generations of Lutherans have learned from the Catechisms economic behaviors that mitigate against greed. But do the Catechisms anticipate social enterprise? Now, what differentiates social enterprise from for-profit corporations or non-profit charities is what is often called the "triple bottom line," namely concern for the planet, people, and profits. Put in different terms, a social enterprise encompasses collective economic behavior that solves some social problem (such as extreme poverty, homelessness, refugees, etc.) with economically sustainable initiatives. To see how the Catechisms might thread this needle between socialist state-sponsored policies and market-based free enterprise we need to turn, as Luther does, from the commandments to the creeds, Lord's Prayer, and sacraments (although I won't have time today to say anything much about Luther on the economics of the sacraments, alas).

Generally speaking, Luther is clear that the commandments teach us "what we ought to do," while the creed and sacraments show us "what God does for us and gives to us" (BC 440). But to interpret this narrowly to limit "what God does" to the visible institution of the church and its rites would be to misunderstand Luther's theology badly. As Luther writes, "we constantly teach that we should see the sacraments and all external things ordained and instituted by God not according to the crude external mask (as we see the shell of a nut) but as that in which God's Word is enclosed" (BC 459). It is grace that saves, through faith, but "faith must have something to believe—something to which it may cling and upon which it may stand" (BC 460). If we distinguish *too* sharply between Law and Gospel, in other words, we do violence to the paradox of the Incarnation. As Luther puts it in his explanation of the second article of the creed in the Small Catechism, using an economic metaphor, Christ "has purchased and freed me." This paradox—to be purchased *and* freed, is what God does for us and gives to us. Such a paradox, I am willing to argue, is also at the heart of social enterprise. Social enterprises attend to the quite real suffering of the planet and people by expressing the human freedom to organize rationally-driven and sustainable economic policies and initiatives. Linking two domains often thought to be separate—people and profits, spirit and flesh, soul and body, social enterprises incorporate in surprising ways (and with often astonishing coalitions and unexpected partnerships) gratitude for our common Gift and engagement on behalf of rational solutions to the problems of human suffering.

We can see how such economic behaviors might flow from the Catechisms especially in Luther's treatment of the first and third articles of the creed, and in his treatment of the fourth petition of the Lord's Prayer. When we confess that "I believe in God, the Father Almighty, creator of heaven and earth," Luther argues in the Small Catechism that we confess that:

> I believe that God has created me together with all that exists. God has given me and still preserves my body and soul: eyes, ears, and all limbs and senses; reason and all mental faculties. In addition, God daily and abundantly

provides shoes and clothing, food and drink, house and farm, spouse and children, fields, livestock and all property—along with all necessities and nourishment for this body and life" (BC 354).

What a remarkably detailed and specific list! Out of it one might draw quite directly policies or enterprises related to physical and mental healthcare, education, clothing and retail, hunger, housing, agriculture, and family law and childcare. Yet again, then, it should be no surprise that in the Large Catechism, Luther's first example of what it means to "believe this article" turns directly to economic life. "If we believed," Luther writes, "we would also act accordingly, and not swagger about and boast and brag as if we had life, riches, power, honor, and such things of ourselves" (BC 433).

In his explanation of the third article of the creed in the Small Catechism, Luther places emphasis on the clause "the community of the saints." In the Large Catechism, he clarifies that what he means by this is "a holy community," which is of course the church, but which he goes on to say "possesses a variety of gifts, and yet is united in love without sect or schism. Of this community I also am a part and member, a participant and co-participant in all the blessings it possesses. I was brought into it by the Holy Spirit and incorporated into it" (BC 437-8). Now, I am neither capable of, nor interested in, a technical parsing of Luther's specific language here. I am interested in his general intent and the *significance* of his language over generations of hearing. And as I hear it, especially in light of our global awareness of religious pluralism and theological and social engagement, we can recognize in what generations of Lutherans have affirmed through study of the third article of the Catechisms is the existence of a community (already, but not yet) gathered in which all stakeholders have a part, and which people are united and yet varied, engaged in works of love, we might put it, without sect or schism. Beyond the imagined communities of state-policies and voluntary organizations, yet through them both, conceivably, happens the actual, and often surprising, work of the Holy Spirit.

Finally, then, we can turn to Luther's interpretation of what it means when we ask God to "give us this day our daily bread." Reiterating his expansive explanation of the first article of the creed, Luther includes among our daily bread "everything included in the necessities and nourishment for our bodies," and then goes on to offer a similar list of examples, including all of the above from the first article and including "upright members of the household, upright and faithful rulers, good government, good weather, peace, health, decency, honor, good friends, faithful neighbors, and the like" (BC 357). Again—what possibilities are laid open in these examples! If it is true, as Luther offers in the Large Catechism, that "the greatest need of all is to pray for the civil authorities and government," we might suggest that in a democratic society where the "government" is of, by, and for the people, Luther's intention would point also to a wide variety of ways in business and public life to give thanks to God for the abundance the earth provides, and to participate in insuring, insofar as possible, justice and peace (BC 450). It is only the devil, as Luther concludes, who "prevents and impedes the establishment of any kind of government or honorable and peaceful relations on earth" (BC 451).

A Third Way and Global Cultural Change that Awaits Our Persuasive Advocacy and Participation

If, historically, Lutherans in Europe have linked the establishment of "honorable and peaceful relations on earth" to government initiatives, in the United States, under the sway of the First Amendment, Lutherans have sought to establish honorable and peaceful relations through political advocacy and through voluntary social ministry organizations. Naturally, I cannot trace all of those links from the sixteenth century to today. But there are dissertations waiting to be written doing just that— tracing the ways Lutheran missionaries worked for greater economic justice and peace in the seventeenth and eighteenth centuries; tracing the ways Lutheran deaconesses promoted healthcare and childcare and in the nineteenth and twentieth centuries; and tracing the ways Lutheran educators, laborers, small business leaders, and artists, and activists of many stripes saw the need to protect the vulnerable and to foster the common good. And—perhaps more importantly for this audience—there are *projects* waiting for capital to develop the kinds of economic behaviors that Luther's Catechisms impel.

It will take creativity to recognize and courage to take the risks to realize the kinds of social enterprises that are implicit in Luther's Catechisms. Doing so will require a turn from clergy-led initiatives to lay-led engagement to solve the complex social problems of education, water-and-food supply, housing, and so many more. There are no blueprints. There is profound need. In the late nineteenth century and the twentieth century, American Lutherans built denominations and social ministry agencies, while German, Swedish, and Danish Lutherans (among others) figured out it was time to stop killing each other and began to build more democratic and just societies. Now, global opportunities await Lutheran engagement in partnership with the kinds of enterprises supported and profiled by Ashoka; the Ethisphere Institute; *Stanford Social Innovation Review,* and many more. Luther's Catechisms leave us, finally, with a legacy of public theology that rests upon the practices of persuasion, empathy, and human capacity-building; of holding each other accountable for the reasons we act in concert. Those Catechisms commit us to practical and theological literacy, to critique of violent economic behavior, and to encouragement of social engagement in economic behaviors that care for the planet, all people, and that prove sustainable.

CHAPTER FIVE

Luther: Forgotten, But Not Gone

Tim Huffman

A funny thing happened to me on the way to visit my late friend Dr. Michael Moeller, a pastor in Wismar, in the northern part of East Germany, then the DDR (German Democratic Republic). Michael had spent a great year with us in Columbus, and I was on a return visit of two weeks. Changing trains and passing through the border formalities as I moved from West to East Berlin, I was pulled aside and put into a small room where I was interrogated for about four hours, missing my connection and leaving Michael to try to figure out what had happened. My offense turned out to be carrying a master's thesis that I had supervised and was giving a final reading on my trip. The thesis by a Lutheran African student was titled something like "Liberation Theology for an African Church." I was questioned and challenged about why I would be bringing "liberation" theology into the DDR. The guards insisted that they did not need liberation, they were already liberated; they implied that I had some subversive purpose for importing this innocent thesis. I finally made my way to Wismar with a good story to tell, though it did not surprise my listeners.

A week later, entering the Luther Museum in Wittenberg, I saw the entrance hall was filled with a display that included a large world map. The map with Wittenberg at its center had arrows radiating in all directions, showing the spread of liberation theology to all parts of the world. The map was insightful in a way that too few had yet understood. Luther's theology has spread far beyond Lutherans, with the focus on liberation in all senses of the word.

History

I wish to affirm everything laid out by my colleagues in the preceding chapters, full of excellent history and theology. I would, however, like to add a couple of historical footnotes, showing that from the very beginning of his life Martin Luther was dealing with economic realities.

Luther was the son of a rough-hewn miner who through arduous work and business deals managed to gain and run a small business mining and smelting copper. His father's work provided daily life lessons for young Martin in the economics of that important business. Remembering that Luther's death came when he was attempting to mediate an economic dispute involving copper mining and the Counts in Mansfeld, it is fair to say that from birth to death Martin Luther was aware of the impact of the economic effects of a large and powerful industry, in which the small miners and smelters were pushed around by the powerful forces of investment banking as well as by church and government authorities.

Another footnote concerns Luther's first and only visit to Rome in 1510-1511. He and another young friar were sent as representatives of seven Observantine monasteries of the German Eremite Augustinian Order to petition their vicar general on monastic business. While there, Luther made pious visits to as many churches, holy places, and relics as time permitted. At one point he wondered whether all the promised indulgences and merits based on various financial fees were true. As time went on, Luther became more and more angry about the corruption he had witnessed in Rome, a corruption with strong economic roots.

By the time of the Ninety-five Theses in 1517, Luther was aware that the church itself openly flouted the biblical and canonical prohibitions of usury. St. Peter's was being built in Rome on money borrowed from the Fugger banking concern of Augsburg, which in turn received annual plenary indulgences granted for the sin of lending at interest to the Vatican.

Despite nearly universal teaching in the U.S., the total proceeds from Tetzel's infamous indulgence sales did *not* go directly for the building of St. Peter's. Half the proceeds went to Rome; the other half went to Albrecht of Brandenburg for repayment of a huge loan and its interest to the Fugger Bank used to finance Albrecht's buying of church positions that included becoming the Archbishop of Mainz. Apart from the issue of bribery for church office, this also was usury at the heart of the church in German lands. So great was Archbishop Albrecht's debt (reports differ on the exact amount), he eventually agreed to abandon the city of Halle to the Protestants when they offered to assume his debt to the Fuggers.

Bribery was also at the heart of the election of young Charles V as Holy Roman Emperor, defeating Luther's patron, the Elector Frederick the Wise. Again, the extensive bribery was financed by a group led by the Fuggers, also representing usury, and that debt would become a huge problem for Charles V and then for the Fuggers themselves.

In addition to his theological objections to indulgences, Luther was indignant that the indulgence sales were taking money from simple German believers to repay the Fuggers for bribes and usurious loans.

Others have pointed out that economics was reflected directly in some of the Ninety-five Theses, a fact often missed by Lutherans reading with only a theological lens. To that we should add that the Ninety-five Theses should be understood as a challenge to the entire systems of economic injustice imposed by the powerful of church and empire on their mostly preliterate and impoverished subjects. Those powerful leaders did not miss the depth and the importance of these challenges, which would ultimately undermine both church and state.

Although Europeans have been more aware of the Fuggers, it is only quite recently that their influence has begun to be appreciated in North America, and it still is absent from most syllabi on the Reformation. It was a surprise when *Business Week* had a full page profile on the Fuggers as "Very (Very, Very) Old Money" in October 2015, following the publication of the book by Greg Steinmetz, *The Richest Man Who Ever Lived: The Life and Times of Jacob Fugger* (Simon and Schuster, 2015). It is worth noting that Luther was barred from attending the Diet at Augsburg in 1530 because the mostly Protestant city of Augsburg would not accept his presence. The leading citizens of Augsburg were the Roman Catholic Fuggers.

Finally, the Fuggers became rich from their mining interests and monopolies, not least a near monopoly in the distribution of copper, which had to affect the Luther family and all German copper miners and smelters. The Peasant Rebellion especially targeted the Fugger mines. Ultimately Fugger funded the Catholic armies attacking the Lutheran Schmalkald League.

Theology

As Lutheran theologians, we have correctly emphasized justification by grace through faith, but we have tended to lose the ineluctable move from justification to justice. This connection—two sides of the same coin—has been the very basis for the theology known as liberation theology, which ironically has tended to be dismissed by northern Lutheran theologians as reductionist, self-justifying, and works righteousness.

Why has the doctrine of justification driven the work of noted liberation theologians, although few of them are Lutherans? Certainly because of its societal and economic consequences.

Let's review the theology. Luther provoked a radical break with the inherited medieval sacramental system. That system had grown increasingly complex, fraught with regulations and stipulations, but with a simple intent—to make people right with God, with the goal of eventual salvation, however long delayed in the near hell of purgatory. And the church existed for and on the money of people desperate to escape the fiery pit, pictured more with images drawn from the medieval Italian poet Dante than from Scripture. Eventually seven sacraments and multiple rites developed, all requiring retinues of clergy and attendants, taking huge amounts of time and money from pious and fearful believers. At the center of all these processes was the medieval church that controlled the toll gates on the road to salvation.

Martin Luther upset the apple cart by discovering the biblical truth that none of this was necessary, that we were and are already right with God, apart from any works, whether religious or secular, because of Christ alone. Thus religious striving, and following all the requirements of a church so obviously corrupt, was a waste of perfectly good time and resources which were given to us by God for God's purposes.

Faith (trust) expresses itself in a radically different way than the medieval sacramental system insisted. Faith is no longer oriented to filling the church's coffers, but becomes active in love, the love of our neighbor, and specifically loving concern for our neighbor in need.

Some liberation theologians have been frank in their dependence on Luther. Protestant liberation theologians include Walter Altmann of Brazil, author of the very important *Luther and Liberation,* with a revised edition just now appearing; Jose Miguez-Bonino of Argentina; Elsa Tamez of Costa Rica; Bishop Medardo Gomez of El Salvador; Michael King Sr., who actually changed his name and that of his young son to Martin Luther King following a visit to Lutherland in Germany.

The Brazilian and former Franciscan Leonardo Boff told me that his famous theology is based on a tripod of authorities: St. Francis, Martin Luther, and Martin Luther King Jr. I responded that it was no wonder he was always in trouble with the Vatican. Carlos Mesters, a Dutch Carmelite missionary to Brazil, worked closely with the Evangelical Church of the Lutheran Confession in Brazil (IECLB) and was a leader of the Bible studies at the Lutheran World Federation Assembly in Curitiba in 1990.

Other Roman Catholic liberationists influenced by Luther have had to avoid his name and even terms like "Reformation" or "reform," at least in public, but have been forthright in identifying "the Pauline doctrine of justification" as the center or the key to understanding their theology. Gustavo Gutierrez, the initiator of the theology of liberation in Latin America, was invited by the University of Lyon to submit his powerful writing as a thesis for a doctorate. In 1985 Gutierrez's journal in Lima, *Paginas,* described the public "interrogation" that was part of the day long process of the university's consideration of his candidacy. Responding to a direct question, Father Gutierrez said, "I consider that the Pauline doctrine of justification is *the* key to understanding my theology, as expressed in *The Theology of Liberation.*" I have discussed this response with him several times, and he affirmed both the words and his commitment to this teaching. It is worth re-reading Gutierrez with this "key" in mind.

Jon Sobrino, the "7th Jesuit," who was out of El Salvador when his colleagues were assassinated by the Atlacatl battalion of the Salvadoran army, worked closely with Lutherans in El Salvador and visited Trinity Lutheran Seminary in Columbus twice, where he was honored along with his slain comrades. He also affirms the centrality of grace as found in Paul's writings. In 2007, after years of close monitoring, the Vatican issued a formal "Notification" condemning aspects of Sobrino's Christology. Sobrino's books on christology are found on the syllabi of many Lutheran seminaries around the world.

Responding to Cardinal Ratzinger's critique in 1984 of liberation theology, the late Jesuit Juan Luis Segundo of Uruguay affirmed the centrality of the Pauline doctrine of justification, at about the same time that his fellow student from the University of Louvain in the 1950s, Gustavo Gutierrez, was making that point in Lyon. In their European studies both had been influenced by the work of Reformed theologians Karl Barth and Jürgen Moltmann, both of whom were nearly Lutheran in their theology, as well as the Lutheran Dietrich Bonhoeffer.

Ernesto Cardenal of Nicaragua, famous as one of the world's top poets and often tipped as a future Nobel winner, is well known for his brilliant five volumes of dialogue sermons, reprinted in one volume as *The Gospel in Solentiname*. But perhaps Cardenal is more famous for the shocking photo of him on his knees on the tarmac of the airport in Managua while being reprimanded by John Paul II for serving as Minister of Culture. Cardenal was stripped of his clerical privileges in 2005 by the Vatican. He has told me of his deep respect for Luther, also cast out by the Vatican.

Intriguingly, Pope Francis, well acquainted with the Lutherans in Argentina, has rehabilitated the word "reform" and applied it to the Vatican Curia itself. The pushback has been severe.

It is both ironic and important in the extreme that the very subjects that Lutherans and Lutheran theologians have tended to miss have been transformative matters for Roman Catholic theologians trying to change the world—all the while being accused of being mere reductionists talking about socio-economic issues.

Some of the best Lutheran theologians in the U.S. have been educated elsewhere, bringing their liberation passion to our shores. Vitor Westhelle and Wanda Deifeldt from Brazil; Willy (Guillermo) Hansen from Argentina; Jose David Rodriguez from Puerto Rico. Quite recently Kirsi I. Stjerna, educated in Finland with her doctorate supervised by Carter Lindberg of Boston University, has written in the new six volume Fortress Series, *The Annotated Luther*: "Luther's theology, just as Luther's spirituality, is about liberation and emancipation by the power of God and God's word. His vision of human life is based on an instinctive sense of equality, per his creation theology, and he applies that in his advice for how to organize human life here in this time and place. His promoting equal opportunity for basic education and his concern for social justice in the form of stressing the importance of taking care of the poor, for instance, is remarkable and something we can—should—pick up today."

The persons I have mentioned are characterized by a deep understanding that justification dare not fail to lead to work for justice and that this includes a challenge to the way things are—to systems that perpetuate class divisions and justify income inequality. We cannot be satisfied that we have said the right things about justification if we have failed to extend that to justice, which must always include economic justice.

In 1984 there was an important conference of Lutheran theologians from North and South America addressing the theme "Justification and

Justice." We re-explored the etymological connection of the two words, agreed that justification is fundamentally making justice or working for justice, and that Lutherans had sometimes gotten justification right but then tended to miss the critical and inescapable move from justification to a commitment to work for justice. It was Vitor Westhelle who laid out for us the beautiful point, which many of us had missed, that working for justice is itself doxology. When we try to rights the wrongs of this world, when we redistribute God's goods, when we reform the economic system, that itself is worship as surely as when we sing "Praise God from whom all blessings flow." There is no contradiction, or even dissonance between feeding the hungry and insisting that all should be fed, and receiving the body and blood of Christ.

How then do we give honor and praise to the God who created us all? Worship? Yes, but what is true worship? Guidance comes from Amos, Micah, and Hosea. We churchy people have a genuine love for the kind of worship that we provide in beautiful buildings with pipe organs and choirs and carefully phrased prayers and proclamation. But remember that Amos brought the word from God, saying:

> I hate, I despise your festivals,
> > And I take no delight in your solemn assemblies.
> Even though you offer me your burnt offerings and grain offerings,
> > I will not accept them;
> And the offerings of well-being of your fatted animals
> > I will not look upon.
> Take away from me the noise of your songs;
> > I will not listen to the melody of your harps.
> But let justice roll down like waters,
> > And righteousness like an ever-flowing stream
> > (Amos 5:21-24 NRSV).

And Micah adds:

> With what shall I come before the Lord
> > and bow down before the exalted God?
> Shall I come before him with burnt offerings,
> > with calves a year old? . . .
> He has shown you, O mortal, what is good.
> > And what does the Lord require of you?
> To act justly and to love mercy
> > and to walk humbly with your God (Micah 6:6-8).

And Hosea shares God's call for repentance, including the words, "For I desire steadfast love and not sacrifice, the knowledge of God rather than burnt offerings" (Hosea 6:6).

Luther in the Small Catechism, on the fifth commandment (You shall not commit murder), enlarges the narrow meaning of the words by explaining, "If you have not fed your hungry neighbor, you have killed him."

Luther's emphasis on service of the neighbor was nicely brought into English by the late George Forell's *Faith Active in Love*. He translates Luther saying, "God does not care even if you never build [God] a church, if you only serve your neighbor." Forell then quotes Luther quoting God, "If you want to love and serve me, do it through your neighbor. He needs your help, I don't."

All of this has been echoed in the lives and work of other native-born citizens of the U.S., like Carter Lindberg, Nelson Trout, Rudolph Featherstone, Jacqueline Bussie, and Mary Jane Haemig.

If this sounds radical, it is. It gets to the very root of Scripture and of Luther's theology, which radically reformed society and economics.

A final group involved in the rediscovery of Luther's significance for the entire world has no apparent interest in "theology," but salutes Luther as the primary initiator of the modern age, overturning the oppressive structures of the medieval world. Not only in Germany, but also in the U.S. the lists compiled by various sources of the most significant persons of the previous millennium, sometimes called "man of the millennium," list Luther as second or third in global significance for the revolutionary effects of his work. And the premier social historian of the west, Jacques Barzun, neither Lutheran nor obviously Christian, begins his magnum opus, *From Dawn to Decadence: 1500 to the Present* (Harper Collins, 2000, 1-2), at the age of ninety-six, with these words:

> The Modern Era begins, characteristically, with a revolution. It is commonly called the Protestant Reformation, but the train of events starting early in the sixteenth century and ending—if indeed it has ended—more than a century later has all the features of a revolution....To call the first of the four revolutions [of the last 500 years] religious is also inadequate...When the miner's son from Saxony...posted his 95 propositions on the door of All Saints church at Wittenberg on October 31, 1517, the last thing he wanted

to do was to break up his church...and divide his world into warring camps.

Yet both happened, as Barzun lays out brilliantly, through Luther's words that we regard as merely theological.

Among the most surprised at these external recognitions of Luther have been Lutherans themselves, possibly because we are "shy," but more likely because we have a reductionist view of Luther as if his only significance is narrowly theological.

Something of a rebuke to Lutherans who have missed Luther's deep social and economic significance, these discoveries of Luther as a true revolutionary should also encourage us to new efforts to speak and work in the public square, and they demonstrate that whether or not the future will include churches or believers known as Lutherans, Luther's revolution, including his deep concern for economic reforms, will continue to be rediscovered as long as people can read.

You will have noticed, I'm sure, that I have been pointing to a movement in the opposite direction from that of most Lutherans. We have imbibed Luther the theologian and teacher, finding truth and meaning in that which the world calls religious. When we are fortunate, we have moved outward from that center to apply Luther the theologian to the realities of the world. But I am suggesting, no *insisting*, that there has been a powerful move from that outside world toward the center of Luther's theology, beginning with the suffering of the world and finding in the monk from Wittenberg the deepest theological grounding for compassion and action, for faith active in love for our neighbor in need. Our role is to see that both directions complete their move toward that unity of action and refection that Latin American theologians call "praxis."

Returning to my opening story, the East German interrogators were right to worry that liberation theology was subversive, a fear found also in the U.S. government at that time. And the Luther Museum display in Wittenberg was right that this subversive liberation theology could be traced from the revolution begun by Brother Martin, with Wittenberg as ground zero for work that would change the world, transforming societies by breaking down the religious justification for monarchy and nobility and classes, ushering in the modern age.

Perhaps we in American Lutheranism can be re-energized by that revolutionary character of our own theological heritage 500 years later, at least enough to situate political debates and economic decisions in a theological and ethical context.

Of itself, that would be a significant contribution to the world, and a fitting legacy of Luther.

A Final Story

Some years ago the world's leading missiologists met for ten days in Buenos Aires with the theme "Economies in Conflict: God or Mammon." With the help of world class economists and political scientists we wrestled with the mission implications of Scripture and church history to understand better the international economic order (IEO). The participants came from all over the world, a profoundly ecumenical and international group from every type of economy. The only thing the group had in common was a deep commitment to the study of the mission of the church in its various forms. Not surprisingly, differences of opinion were voiced. As I wrote later, about 135 leading Christian scholars of mission eventually sorted into two contending conclusions. About one half asserted that the IEO is idolatrous, a clearly critical perspective. The other half argued, "No, the IEO is not idolatrous. It is actively demonic."

Idolatrous or demonic? Is that too radical a judgment? In the language of seminarians, will it preach? Or translated for church professionals, will it pass at an assembly?

Listening to the work presented by the fine colleagues preceding me persuades me that Brother Martin would have less trouble with such judgments that the average person bearing his name today.

It requires many skills to impact the IEO. Those with their hands on the levers of power routinely try to intimidate people of faith away from any involvement. Witness the vitriolic reaction against Pope Francis and his criticism of the IEO and of capitalism.

But if the world's missiologists are right that the IEO is either idolatrous or demonic, it is precisely people of faith who are needed to expose what is really happening.

Unless the missiologists are wrong, we are in a crisis.

And a crisis is a terrible thing to waste.

CHAPTER SIX

A New Vision

Ryan P. Cumming

Jesus went on with his disciples to the villages of Caesarea Philippi; and on the way he asked his disciples, "Who do people say that I am?"And they answered him, "John the Baptist; and others, Elijah; and still others, one of the prophets." He asked them, "But who do you say that I am?" Peter answered him, "You are the Christ" (Mark 8:27-29).

Jesus' question and Simon Peter's response are in all three of the synoptic gospels—Matthew, Mark, and Luke—and in all three versions the episode is riddled with allusions to the connections between faith and perception. In Mark's gospel, this is made clearer by a rather unsubtle miracle. Just in case the readers of the gospel don't quite get it, Mark makes the importance of perception, "sight," obvious by including Jesus' healing of a blind man in Bethsaida:

He took the blind man by the hand and led him out of the village; and when he had put saliva on his eyes and laid his hands on him, he asked him, "Can you see anything?" And the man looked up and said, "I can see people, but they look like trees, walking." Then Jesus laid his hands on his eyes again; and he looked intently and his sight was restored, and he saw everything clearly (Mark 8:23-25).

The point the gospels make here is not unique—"right" faith begets "right" sight. Faith is not merely a matter of believing but of perceiving. Faith is a lens through which the disciples see Christ and through which they—and we—see the world. Even among other biblical authors, this is clear. Consider Paul's contrast between sight and blindness in his second letter to the Corinthians: "In their case the god of this world has blinded the minds of the unbelievers, to keep them from seeing the light of the Gospel of the glory of Christ, who is the image of God" (2 Corinthians 4:4). To have faith is to see in a particular way. To have faith that is well-founded is to have clear sight.

Jesus' question interrogates the disciples' faith. If Peter is the norm, they have the belief part down pat: "You are the Christ." But faith is not merely a matter of orthodoxy, of believing. It is a matter of seeing. When Peter is unable to grasp the vision Jesus lays out for what human life has in store for the Christ (Mark 8:32), it is clear that he is unable to see through the lens of faith. And Jesus rebukes him. "Who do you say that I am?" is another way of asking, "What do you see when you see me?"

This question of seeing is the very foundation of the Christian life, indeed of the moral life, in general. The values we hold dear, the moral choices we make, at their root depend on how we see the world, how we see ourselves, and how we see God. Philosopher Arne Johan Vetleson argues that perception is crucial to action. If we act immorally, Vetleson says, it's not necessarily because we don't know how to make good choices. It's often because we failed to see things the right way.[1]

Seeing is especially important when it comes to what's called social ethics. Social ethics deals with questions about how society is organized and how institutions like government or the economy shape the lives of individuals and communities. Lutheran theologian James Childs argues that perception—especially "the way we see ourselves"—is critical to "the shaping of our structures of justice."[2] The decisions we make, the policies we enact, and the way our social institutions—schools, government, the economy, even the church—run depend largely on how we see ourselves and one another. Any large changes to these institutions likewise begin with a dramatic change in perception, with a new "lens" to look through.[3]

Consider, for example, the dramatic changes in government responses to poverty between the 1960s and the 1980s. In 1964, President Lyndon Johnson declared "unconditional war on poverty" and enjoyed support for the numerous initiatives this would create, including Medicare, Medicaid, permanent establishment of the food stamp program, and the Head Start program. Many Americans were driven by the images of poverty presented in Michael Harrington's popular 1962 study of domestic poverty, *The Other America*, to support a more robust response from government to poverty. This continued into the 1970s.But by the late 1980s, spending on social programs like welfare[4] was drastically cut, and by the mid-1990s welfare as Americans had known it for half a century was gone.

How did such a dramatic shift happen? One explanation is an equally dramatic transformation in how Americans viewed their neighbors in poverty. In a fascinating analysis, Laurie MacLeod, Darrel Montero, and Alan Speer tracked the changes in American attitudes toward welfare and welfare recipients from 1938 to 1995. The authors note that "the percentage of those who agreed that the government has a responsibility to provide for the poor shifted slightly downward" between 1985 and 1997.[5] One of the explanations for this is "the public's increasing resentment and disdain for the poor today."[6] Indeed, while most attitudes of Americans stayed fairly consistent from the 1930s to the 1990s, the authors found one notable exception: "a growing percentage of Americans believe that welfare recipients are to blame for their poverty."[7]

Law professor Ann Cammett believes that this change in perception laid the groundwork for the dismantling of welfare under Presidents Ronald Reagan and Bill Clinton. She describes how the images of "welfare queens" and "deadbeat dads" came to shape how Americans viewed people in poverty in the 1980s. Gone were the images of the "deserving poor." In the rhetoric of the 1980s, "the poor" came to be seen as lazy and dishonest, getting fat off the government calf. As this new lens took hold, opposition to government spending for means-tested programs like welfare grew until finally, in 1996, Clinton obliterated what was once known as welfare in favor of the strict and severely limited Temporary Assistance to Needy Families.

In retrospect, we now know that the image of the "welfare queen" was far removed from reality, but it's too late. Welfare is already gone. The goal of remaking the system of cash assistance to people in poverty was accomplished by a shift in perception of people in poverty. Once people in poverty were seen widely as lazy or undeserving, the American public also came to see welfare as an unfair benefit that awarded poor choices or enabled immoral activity. How Americans viewed people in poverty shaped what they saw as just and fair policies.

Why this lengthy reflection on perception? Because to a large extent, what the authors in this book argue is that our world is in need of a different lens through which to see the economy and our communities. They argue that Lutherans in particular have this lens to offer, even if it needs to be dusted off a bit.

A Lutheran Lens

Lutherans affirm that faith does not give Christians some sort of special knowledge about how to organize a society. (We have some good ideas, though!) But Lutherans do acknowledge that faith gives us a particular perspective on how an economy or a government ought to function and the goals either ought to serve. Martin Luther exemplified this perspective with what we might call his "reforming eye." This reforming eye was a way of seeing the world critically and discerning how institutions like the economy, government, and especially the church, fared against two important questions. First, how well does this institution reflect the intentions of God as revealed in Scripture and, second, how does this institution affect my neighbor, especially the most vulnerable neighbor? This perspective means asking difficult questions and being prepared for disappointing answers.

History has well-documented what Luther saw when he looked at the medieval Catholic Church—an institution that preyed on the vulnerable by selling worthless indulgences to finance new construction. Less well-known, however, is what this perspective meant for how Luther viewed the economy and what this Lutheran lens, detailed so well in the preceding chapters, means for Lutherans today. As we will see, this Lutheran lens is the critical difference between ministry that *responds* to problems and ministry that *solves* them. As such, it is vastly important, particularly, for the anti-hunger and anti-poverty ministries of the Lutheran church. To respond to immediate needs of people facing hunger and poverty is critical work in the short-term. But without a view that encompasses the array of causes, we will only be treating the symptoms.

An illustration might be helpful. A man gathers boxes of cereals and cans off shelves to fill his small basket. As he rounds the corner of the aisle, he snags one of the last jars of peanut butter. Last, he adds a small pack of diapers to his cache before greeting a woman with a nametag near the exit. She helps him bag his items and smiles as he utters his clear and heartfelt thanks. She watches him go, knowing that in a week or a month, he will be back for more.

Scenes like this play out in food pantries all over the U.S., especially in what are known as "choice" pantries, where clients are able to "shop" for donated goods as if they were at a store. And for all intents and purposes, there is nothing that makes this man seem any different from an everyday customer at a store, but for the facility in which he does his shopping.

"What do you see when you see me?"

"Who do you say that I am?"

Superficially, we could use vague terms to describe the man and his poverty: unfortunate, down-on-his-luck, in a rough patch. But dig a little deeper and the picture becomes both clearer and infinitely more complicated. Woven into his story is a young daughter, recently diagnosed with a severe, chronic illness. Another thread reveals a full-time, minimum wage job with no sick leave—a job he lost for taking too much time off to care for his child.[8] Another thread bears echoes of phone calls from billing departments, demanding payment for medical treatments.[9] Perhaps another reveals a criminal conviction for a minor drug crime when he was nineteen, a mark that still closes doors to jobs even now, twenty years later.[10] Another thread: the high cost of rent that prevents saving for a rainy day.[11] Another thread: the reduction in SNAP[12] benefits his state enacted last year. And another and another and so on.

"What do you see when you see me?"

There is nothing unusual in this tapestry. Anyone who has worked in hunger relief ministries for a good amount of time can tell stories like this, stories of unemployment, criminal records, mental illness, health care expenses, and the like. Relief ministries—food pantries, community meals, backpack programs for children, etc.—exist at the intersection of systems and policies that shape our lives in significant ways. It is no wonder, then, that ELCA World Hunger, the signature expression of the ELCA's response to hunger and poverty, is also one of the principal ministries of the church with and among people impacted by the criminal justice system, health care systems, and even climate change. Each of these plays a huge role in the ability of people in the U.S. and around the world to provide for themselves and their families.

One of the more popular ways to describe these underlying systems is as "root causes" of hunger. This metaphor, though pithy, implies that with enough knowledge, we can pinpoint the several issues that, once solved, will eliminate the problem of hunger. Unfortunately, the reality is more complex than this. A better image might not be a series of "roots" but one massive, twisted "root ball," a gnarled collection of systems that intersect with each other at various points. The vulnerability that leads someone to the door of a food pantry very rarely has one clear cause. More typically, it involves multiple causes: mental illness *and* unemployment, low wages *and* high rent.

Relief ministries encounter people within these intersections. As they respond to the immediate needs of clients, volunteers and staff are also responding to the often-hidden consequences of how large systems like the economy and the government are structured. Whether we recognize it or not, relief is never "merely" charity; it is a witness to the shortcomings of our conceptions of justice.

The problem if we don't recognize this is that relief can enable injustice to continue. Simon Peter's failure was his inability to recognize that being embodied meant being vulnerable—to the Sanhedrin, to Herod, to Pilate, to the cross. And it was a failure to see how God might turn that vulnerability into power. Relief remains the most prominent response of Lutherans to hunger and poverty, but it also remains perhaps the most vulnerable to a failing vision that misses the tangled systems that underlie hunger and poverty.

When relief is done right, when it is shaped by clear perception of these underlying systems, it can be a powerful expression of justice. At a park in the Bay Area of California, a Lutheran congregation worships and hosts a community meal with homeless men and women. Together they pray, they sing, they commune, and they dine. This Sunday afternoon gathering may not by itself solve the region's housing crisis. But it is a prophetic testimony against policies and attitudes that ignore the problem of homelessness and deny the humanity of people who are homeless.

Compare this to relief rooted in a malformed perception of people in need. In a conversation some time ago, a fellow Lutheran described to me the standard practice at a food pantry near her church. Each visit, a client receives a single bag of groceries for the week. For many, this is enough to help them ensure healthy meals for their families. After several visits, though, a staff person at the pantry typically asks the client for an explanation of their poverty. Many clients are sent away at that point with their bag of groceries and the stern advice that they should move to an area they can afford, since they are clearly living outside their means.

On the surface, both the community meal and the pantry are doing similar things—providing food to those in need. But clearly, the people operating each ministry have very different perceptions of the participants in their ministries. At the community meal, people who are homeless are welcomed as neighbors, as people at the mercy of economic forces and real estate markets they do not control, yet nonetheless as people with a right to be part of the community. At the food pantry, clients are viewed as dependents, as people who have made the wrong choices about where to live and who have not earned the right to be part of the community. At the pantry, the cost of housing is accepted as a given, and people without sufficient means must learn to adapt by moving. At the park, the cost of housing is understood as part of the "root ball" of causes of hunger that threatens community rather than characterizes it. Both ministries relieve hunger, but only one is rooted in a vision that might ultimately end it.

Charity vs. Justice

The need for this new (or renewed) vision to end hunger and poverty has been at the center of a growing debate between relief and development, or in terms more familiar to Christians, between charity and justice. The argument goes something like this: relief ministries that only meet immediate needs don't address root causes of poverty. What is more, they undermine solutions by creating dependency and, still worse, they are nearly always paternalistic and deprive needy people of their dignity. Thus, they are a waste of precious resources that would be better spent on sustainable development. Charity, the argument goes, does not work.

Two of the more popular books that have gained traction among people of faith are *Toxic Charity* by Robert D. Lupton and *When Helping Hurts* by Steve Corbett and Brian Fikkert.[13] To some extent, the critique they both offer is incredibly important, and the stories they recount of charity gone wrong accurately reflect real shortcomings of volunteerism and ministry, especially of the "mission trip" stripe. Lupton, for example, tells of the volunteers who inexpertly laid tile in a Cuban seminary while local, skilled laborers were denied the chance to do the work for pay. He describes Christmas gift-giving to children that left fathers feeling emasculated and of the Mexican wall that was painted six times by six different mission groups one summer. The stories reflect what happens when well-intentioned action is divorced from well-formed perception. The hearts of the volunteers in Cuba were in the right place, but their eyes were closed to the fact that the community needed opportunities for paid work a whole lot more than they needed a tile floor. They failed to see their work in the context of local unemployment. Thus, they failed to ask the right questions: Why is there poverty in this community? How will our work help address this?

I recall a similar story much closer to (my) home. Take a drive through southwest Detroit, and you'll see a vibrant, growing community, but you'll also see one filled with vacant, overgrown lots littered with trash. To someone from the suburbs around Detroit, this blight is unconscionable. Their desire to beautify the city is understandable. A friend at a congregation in Detroit described to me her frustration, though, at the numerous suburban groups who ask if they can visit and do service by clearing the vacant lots. They can't understand why my friend tries to dissuade them.

Their hearts may be in the right place, but again, their vision is too narrow. They see a dirty lot and think the problem is litter. What they don't see when they look at that lot is an absentee landlord failing to follow the law and take care of his or her property. What they do not see is a whole network of irresponsible (mostly wealthy and absentee) landowners letting neighborhoods go to seed because they just don't give a damn. The problem is not litter; it is accountability. And since they don't see this, they don't see that clearing the property removes the only leverage the community has to pressure the city to enforce property maintenance laws.

They also miss the way in which their activity, their "cleaning up," can reflect a negative perception of the people in these communities. Detroit is not "dirty" because its residents do not care; often, the city's people are too busy working as landscapers, maintenance workers, and maids in upscale suburbs to have time to dedicate to their own city. Correcting this means moving from "What can we do to clean up Detroit?" to "What economic forces make our neighborhood look different from one in Detroit?"

Authentic, effective ministry demands authentic, comprehensive vision. This is an important critique Lupton, Corbett, and Fikkert offer. Yet like the old adage from Matthew, at the same time, they fail to see the "log" in their own eyes. The solution to "helping" that "hurts," for Corbett and Fikkert, is a comprehensive strategy for development. Some of their suggestions are worth hearing, but part of the comprehensive picture of poverty they paint is the belief that people in poverty lack not only material resources but also, importantly, faith. Thus, according to the authors, real poverty alleviation includes helping people in poverty gain a renewed faith, since a lack of faith is part of what keeps them materially poor.

This nonsensical argument unfortunately undermines their whole proposal. Faith can do a lot of things, but it cannot magically make a person less vulnerable to market forces that affect employment or real estate trends that increase rents or health care changes that drive up costs. The author's perception of poverty as a consequence of deficient faith is marred by a major blindspot, one that misses a key reality of our current economic situation: faithful or not, we are all at risk.

Like Corbett and Fikkert, Lupton, too, casts a vision that is myopic. Lupton's shortsightedness does not arise from a view limited by evangelical faith but from an insufficient perspective on what makes us human. For him, the basic problem of poverty is that people in need are unable or unwilling to participate in the current economy and most charity doesn't help this. Instead, "toxic charity" enables people to become too dependent and not self-sufficient. Self-sufficiency, he argues, is the foundation of human dignity, dignity often denied to recipients of charity.

Lupton raises an important critique, but again, the vision here misses the point on two counts. First, he fails to see that self-sufficiency is not a defining characteristic of human beings. We are, if anything, *dependent* creatures. Even the most ardent capitalist knows that the whole existence of the market is based on the idea that we need each other. The clothesmaker needs the farmer to grow the food he will purchase. The farmer needs the manufacturer to make the tractor to plow his fields. The manufacturer needs the construction worker to maintain the roads her trucks will use for shipping, and so on. To miss this wide web of dependence and declare that the dignified life is a self-sufficient one sets ministry up for failure!

This points to the second thing Lupton ignores, which is that our dependence makes us vulnerable, particularly when we have little control over the systems on which we depend or little participation in shaping them. Certainly, ministries that focus on sustainable development rather than relief are vastly important. Vocational programs, education, and the like have proven quite successful in helping people out of poverty. But what good is a job training program in an economy where fewer and fewer jobs pay a living wage? Or, what of our hypothetical food pantry client above? In New Jersey, Lutheran Episcopal Advocacy Ministry of New Jersey (LEAM-NJ) has been working to secure paid sick leave for full-time employees because so many run into problems similar to his situation, losing their pay or their jobs because of medical emergencies. Participation in the economy is certainly a good thing, but it does not mean our work is done. Merely getting hired does not magically solve larger problems, like wage theft, a lack of worker protections, or depressed wages.

An aspect missing from the discussion is what has been called "structural injustice." This kind of injustice includes the ways that opportunities are open or closed in different ways to different people. Structural injustice is present when one group of people, such as people with wealth or people who are identified as white, have more access to opportunities than another group, such as people in poverty or persons of color.[14]

The hard part of dealing with structural injustice is that it is deeply entrenched, and there is not necessarily one individual or group to blame. It's one thing if an employer acts unfairly. It's easy to see how that situation might be corrected (though not necessarily easy to correct)! Structural injustice, though, is sometimes harder to see and harder to correct, partly because we're so enmeshed in it that it can be hard to extricate ourselves from it.

An example of the binding power of structural injustice might be helpful. At a large event, a variety of ministries hosted exhibits in an indoor space. For those on the inside, this was a chance to introduce thousands of people to the work the church does around the world and the ways that they are part of this work. Yet, space was not available to everyone. Stitching up Detroit (SuD), a collective of youth from Detroit who design and hand-screen t-shirts, were relegated to a small patio outside of the venue, out of view of most attendees. As a program focused on developing marketable skills among creative young people, skills that could lead to full-time work once they become adults, SuD would seem to be a shining example to highlight the development work the ELCA supports in distressed communities. Yet, they were excluded from participating fully in the market this event created. Why?

There was no conscious decision to exclude them. The organizers of the event did everything they could to lift up local ministries and programs. Had there been an opportunity, they likely would have done more. Uncovering the source of SuD's economic marginalization means wading through interconnected systems: expo center fees that are too high for small enterprises, exclusive vendor contracts that protect larger vendors, local ordinances that require licensing, etc. These systems together formed a structure that left SuD marginalized from the best economic opportunities it hopes to open up for youth in Detroit. This is what is meant by structural injustice. Even if some of the other larger vendors would have financially helped SuD gain space indoors, this would not have been "justice" but patronage. The favoring of vendors with large amounts of capital, visibility, and connections—the kind of economic power start-ups and small businesses often lack—is not limited to events but is an undercurrent in the economic system more broadly. No amount of superficial charity will correct this. Nor will any ministry that fails to see it be able to address the poverty and hunger this injustice creates.

All that said, it does not seem apparent that charity needs to be cast aside so much as re-defined. There is a difference between the sort of harmful charity that might be better considered patronage and the kind of charity that itself can be justice-seeking. One of the reasons the vision of structural injustice is so hard to grasp is that if we really internalize what we see, we are compelled to make changes that demand sacrifice. In his moving poem, "Archaic Torso of Apollo," Rainer Maria Rilke reflects on the classical sculpture of the Greek god Apollo, a sculpture that captivates him, draws him in, and challenges him. He concludes that once grasped by the fullness of power in the piece of art, he is left without another choice: "You must change your life." Social justice advocates refer to this process as "conscientization," the awakening of our conscience, and it is a critical step in the movement toward economic justice. Once we really see structural injustice, we are grasped by it and there is no other choice: "You must change your life." If we aren't moved to that level of awareness, our conscience is still asleep.

Re-defining charity means taking seriously the power of a ministry to be a place where agency for change can be nurtured. Charity as an activity that happens after we are formed as members of a faith community must give way to charity as an integral part of this formation. A relief ministry that provides food is a good thing. But it is a "charitable" thing inasmuch as it forms us to be charitable people in the literal sense of "charity" as *caritas*—love. Charity, as William

Cavanaugh points out, is not the activity of giving but a way of orienting our whole existence towards the good of the neighbor. When this focus is wedded to a vision that encompasses the unjust systems that bind the neighbor (and ourselves!), we cannot help but become "conscientized" to seek justice. The line between "justice" and "charity" blurs, and we see that separating them—believing that charity can still be a good thing absent economic justice—becomes, as Cavanaugh describes it an "impediment to seeing reality as God sees it."[15]

The model of charity, for Christians, is the free gift of Christ to a people who were undeserving. Yet, in this gift is God's testimony not only for the salvation of God's people but against all that threatens God's people—all the Sanhedrins, the Herods, the Pilates, and the crosses. It is a model of charity as a gift to people (us) who can't help themselves, sure, but it is also a testimony that this kind of vulnerability should not be. The injustice that allows crosses to be planted on Mt. Calvary—and allows so many "crosses" to be planted in distressed communities today—is uncovered and opposed by the free gift of Christ. It may be "charity," but it is "toxic" only to those who would perpetuate injustice.

Casting a New Vision

What ties this example to the essays in this book is this penetrating vision of structural injustice. Each of the authors, in their own way, argues that a similar dynamic is at work throughout our entire economy. Though he never used the term "structural injustice," Luther was aware of the ways the economy in his day left a few people very well-off and the vast majority of people impoverished. It's this critique that the authors here bring to bear on our own day. And the facts bear them out.

In 2014, 46.7 million Americans (about 14.8 percent of the population) were living in poverty, meaning that their household income was below the national poverty threshold. For a family of four, this means their annual income was below $23,850. That same year, 48.1 million Americans experienced food insecurity, meaning there were times when they were not sure where their next meal might come from. For nearly one million children, this was a frequent experience. Around the world, 795 million people were undernourished in 2014. This is a huge decrease from previous decades, but it still represents about one in nine people globally, and progress on this has slowed. The World Economic Forum notes that increasing income inequality is one of the "key challenges" of our time. "In developed and developing countries, the poorest half of the population often controls less than 10 pecent of its wealth."[16] In the United States, the top 20 percent of households own more than 80 percent of the nation's wealth, while the bottom 40 percent of households own less than 0.3 percent. Real wages among most workers in the U.S. have fallen since 2000, while wages for the wealthiest Americans have risen nearly 10 percent.[17]

Against this disenchanting reality, the authors propose a recovery of a Lutheran perspective on the economy, a perspective that can refine the church's anti-hunger and anti-poverty ministry and serve as a source for an alternative economic witness. This is particularly true for the ELCA's numerous hunger relief programs, which represent the vast majority of ways the ELCA responds to hunger in the U.S. As described above, these ministries exist at the intersection of a multitude of systems. As such, they are on the frontlines of the clash between the economy as it is and the economy as Lutherans believe it ought to be. What remains for us here is to draw some conclusions from our Lutheran heritage as detailed by the other authors in this book and to suggest what these might mean practically today.

Economy of Grace vs. Economy of Merit

The reality of our current economy is that it is very hard to get ahead and very easy to fall behind. Those who have done ministry with and among people in poverty see what Samuel Torvend describes as "the darkest side of the economic system in which we live. . . . All boats have not risen. In fact, many have capsized."[18] Gordon Huffman agrees, highlighting the deep division between the haves and the have-nots:

> We have a society where it's not true that rising tides lift all boats. And the question is to what degree do we want to become a barricaded society . . . where those who have [wealth] . . . put gates around their communities and bars on their windows. That's not a healthy way to live.[19]

One of the principal arguments in support of the current capitalist economy in the U.S. is that the benefits accrue to those who most deserve them. This has long been the dominant narrative of the American economy. Those who work hard and make good choices accrue wealth. Poverty, in this narrative, is understood as the result of poor choices and actions. Perhaps it's laziness, or a failure to plan wisely, or a series of bad decisions, but whatever the cause, a person is in poverty because they have not earned the right to enjoy all the fruits the economy has to offer. Recall what was said above about "welfare queens" and the changing perception of poverty. If people in poverty are viewed as "undeserving," then the rest of us feel quite comfortable when the economy and the government leaves them behind. Detractors, of course, point to the numerous cases where, more than anything, rotten luck leads to poverty. Or, they highlight the especially tragic cases where a person had no choice, such as in situations of intimate partner violence that inhibit the economic opportunities available to victims.[20]

From a Lutheran perspective, which acknowledges grace as the basic animating principle of the world God has created, the debate itself is wrongheaded from the start. This debate assumes that the economy at its core is intended to function as a system of rewards and punishments. The hard-working are rewarded. The lazy are punished. The retort from detractors often superficially stops at this level. Their response is that the system of rewards and punishments regulated by the economy is not functioning well, since so many deserving people are not rewarded. Less frequently does their critique draw into question whether the economy ought to be founded on a system of merit at all.

This is where a Lutheran perspective can be particularly helpful and particularly challenging. As Lutherans, we believe that God has great plans for our future, for a time when the fullness of the Gospel will come to fruition under God's perfect reign. But until that time, God has instituted certain systems that allow us to live—and to live well—this side of paradise. Recognizing the need for nurturing care and education, God gives us the family. Understanding the reality of threats to our safety and the need to organize our common life, God has given us government. Of course, as we know, when it comes to how these gifts are shaped by humans, they are far from perfect. Yet, they remain gifts of God, and we can recognize their imperfections, in part, because of our discernment of God's intentions for these institutions and because we share the gift of reason that helps us distinguish justice from injustice, fairness from unfairness.

For Luther, each of these institutions is purposeful, which means they each have an end toward which God has created them. They are also limited, which means they have boundaries on their activity that ought not to be crossed. Government, for example, exists to protect us from injustice and to organize common life. It is not meant to interfere with our faith. That falls under the auspices of another order, namely the church. Nor is government meant to replace the family. It may, however, step in if family dynamics put an individual's safety at risk, like in cases of abuse.

The key point, though, is that these institutions are not meant to constrain life but to enable it. Through them, we are empowered to express our faith, practice love of neighbor, and experience the ever-present grace of God. The economy is no exception. As one of these "orders of creation," Luther understands the economy as a gift of God through which we fulfill our vocations and, by so doing, meet our needs and serve one another.

Here is where the Lutheran perspective runs up against an economy of merit. Lutheran faith is rooted in the belief that both our salvation and our existence are made possible by the free gift of God. Apart from anything we have done to deserve it, God sustains and saves us through grace. For Lutherans, grace is the basic way God relates to the world. This runs strictly counter to systems of faith rooted in notions of merit or reward and punishment. The Lutheran view of the economy as an expression of God's grace—a gift –intended for our well-being now, prior to the full experience of God's reign, lays the groundwork for an alternative vision of the right goals of the economy. The basic principle that ought to shape our relationship to the economy is not merit but grace.

It is far too simplistic to dismiss this alternative witness as merely claiming that everything bought and sold on the market ought instead to be free, or to say that no one should have to work. Indeed, work, our daily vocation, was understood by Luther to be a key way that Christians fulfill their calling to love and serve the neighbor. A baker, for instance, loves and serves the neighbor not by quitting work but by doing it and so making bread available to the community. Luther's critique of the economy was not the mere process of buying and selling but rather the rapaciousness of merchants who sold their goods at prices too "dear." The economy, Luther argued, encouraged people to see vocation as merely the pursuit of profit, rather than as an expression of neighbor-love.

In an economy of grace, the goal is the well-being of all members of a community. It is rooted in mutual dependence and a sense of calling, not a competition for rewards. Of course, such an economic vision, Helen Rhee argues, can act as "leaven" in the world, since it "foster[s] greater sensitivity to the works and vision of justice and serves as a witness to God's creative intention and purpose: the common good and well-being of all people and of the creation."[21] This inspires a commitment to both charity and justice and the re-shaping of structures and systems so that "all people [can] contribute their talents and creativity to the common good."[22]

This means that, for Lutherans, the question is not whether our economy efficiently and consistently responds to an individual's merit but rather whether our economy is structured such that all can participate and share in the goods necessary for life. Any other view of the economy, in essence, is based on a belief that the world God has created is based on merit, not grace. This belief in merit isn't just a difference of opinion. For Lutherans, it's a denial of the Gospel.

The importance of "Why?"

Picking apart the "root ball" of hunger demands a critical lens. It means asking the hard questions about the causes of hunger and poverty and being prepared to act on the answers. Lutherans are well-equipped for this. "The Lutheran tradition," Torvend says, "grew out of asking difficult questions, and these difficult questions brought about reform."[23] Recall Luther's "reforming eye" described above. The Reformer didn't accept the status quo of passive agreement to papal edicts. Rather, he interrogated the institutions of his day, particularly on the question of how vulnerable people fared under institutional practices and policies. He asked the hard questions about the use and abuse of power, questions we are called to ask today.

"To be sure," Carter Lindberg notes in his essay above, "the biblical mandate to feed the poor is non-controversial. What is controversial is why people are poor and hungry."[24] When we start asking these questions, we bring justice together with charity. Again, from Torvend: ". . . in addition to charitable response is discerning why people . . . are suffering in the first place. And that moves us from charitable giving . . . into asking the larger question, which is, 'why is there injustice? What is it within the larger system in which people live that produces this kind of suffering?'"[25]

For all their faults, Corbett, Fikkert, and Lupton are at least raising these questions. Their shortcomings are having answers that are too narrow. One of the benefits of the chapters in this book is reminding Lutherans of "the Luther who throughout his life excoriated an unregulated profit economy and created social progress."[26] Jon Pahl's treatment of the Lutheran catechisms, for example, sheds light on the ways Lutherans are called to see themselves as part of the economy and to examine critically what this means for our neighbors. This is essential for authentic ministry. It does little good to believe that God's word calls us to respond to hunger through a congregational food pantry if we, at the same time, do nothing about the economic policies that keep that pantry stocked with clients.

Relief ministries, again, are on the frontlines here. They are the sites where we learn more about the structures and systems that bring clients to the doors. By listening to clients' stories, we refine our critical lens for a better understanding of the problems and clearer vision for solutions. This listening isn't rooted in the contentious "why?" asked by the staff at the food pantry described earlier. It is the "why" of accompaniment that listens to the neighbors' story so that we can better enter into it.

Of course, at the same time, relief ministries must be sites where we are free to be self-critical about how we enter into these stories. In a visit to Colombia, colleagues and I spent time in the Sierra Nevada Mountains with the Kogui, an indigenous community whom ELCA World Hunger accompanies through our relationship with the Evangelical Lutheran Church in Colombia (*Iglesia Evangelico Luterana de Colombia*). In one conversation, a member of the community told us of another church that used to ship food to some of the Kogui families. Over time, the families became dependent on the food and reduced their own farming. As a result, they lost the knowledge they needed to successfully farm the difficult terrain of the mountainside. Because of this, the Kogui agreed as a community to refuse this kind of aid in the future. While immediately helpful, the U.S.-based church providing the food failed to ask critically what structures lay under the Kogui's hunger and how their aid addressed this. Had they asked, "Why?" they may have heard about the need for land and the need for community as part and parcel of the need for food. Instead, their charity was not only ineffective but harmful.

Building relationships, not programs

This points to another insight gleaned from the earlier chapters: the importance of relationships. The Lutheran understanding of the economy begins with the affirmation of our mutual dependence on one another and on God. When functioning well, this dependence strengthens communities. When functioning poorly, it divides them. Aware of this, two other important questions we need to ask are whether our economy enables the formation of healthy communities, and whether our anti-hunger ministries participate in this. Part of the creation of community is recognizing the need for our ministries to be sites where relationships are formed and not just facilities where goods are distributed.

Another way of getting at this question is to discern what goals are reflected in our activities. Is the goal ending hunger? Or, is the goal ensuring all are fed? These are two very different goals. In the first, the focus is on a problem—lack of food. Any system of food distribution can be part of this. But in the second, the focus is not on a problem but on a person. Ensuring all are fed recognizes the many faces of "hunger"—for food, for fellowship, for identity, for community— and reflects the understanding that we all are in mutual need. It also reflects a commitment to accompanying one another and listening to one another as we discern our needs together. This is one reason why ELCA World Hunger has not adopted the term "food security" as part of its mission, despite the popularity of food security in research and reports from other organizations and agencies. "Food security" doesn't capture the expansive set of needs we have in mind when we talk about "hunger," nor does it adequately capture the comprehensive ministries ELCA World Hunger supports.

Shobi's Table, an ELCA ministry in St. Paul, Minnesota, is a good example of a ministry focused on relationships. Through a mobile food truck, Pastor Margaret Kelly and a core group of volunteers distribute food to poor and homeless people in their community. The ministry, though, involves more than just charitable distribution. "The aim," Rev. Kelly says, "is to empower the community." This means accompanying people where they are and responding to a variety of hungers. Certainly, people hunger for food. But they also "are deeply hungry for prayer [and] to be known, to be seen."[27] These are manifestations of hunger that exist when the economy marginalizes people, and they are forms of hunger that can only be met by building relationships.

The "liturgy after the liturgy"

Another insight that comes from the Lutheran tradition is that worship and service are intimately connected. One of the common threads found in the previous chapters is that Luther's economic vision was lost to history, in part, because Lutherans for so long emphasized piety over praxis, the interior spirituality of faith over the service of the neighbor to which that faith calls us. As the other authors have persuasively argued, this division between the church as worshiping presence and the church as liberating presence is not an accurate reflection of what the church is called to be.

In this bifurcation, we lose touch with the picture of worship reflected not only in Luther's works but in Scripture. The consistent witness in Scripture is that the only authentic worship is worship done by a community that authentically loves and serves the neighbor with justice. To put it another way, without justice, there is no worship. Isaiah commends this in regards to fasting: "Is this not the fast I choose: to loose the bonds of injustice, to undo the thongs of the yoke, to let the oppressed go free...to share your bread with the hungry and bring the homeless poor into your house?" (Isaiah 58:6-7). Amos highlights this, too, at least in the negative. He excoriates Israel for its economic inequality and inequity in its justice system and ties these to God's judgment: "I hate, I despise your feasts, and I take no delight in your assemblies. . . . I will not accept your offerings. . . . take away from me the noise of your songs. . . . I will not listen" (Amos 5:21-23). Even Micah, whose famous verse progressive Christians love to quote, focuses his prophecies on worship:

> With what shall I come before the Lord, and bow myself before God on high? Shall I come before him with burnt offerings, with calves a year old? Will the Lord be pleased with thousands of rams, with ten thousands rivers of oil? He has showed you, O mortal, what is good, and what does the Lord require of you but to do justice and to love kindness and to walk humbly with your God?" (Micah 6:6-8).

This isn't a verse about social concern; it's about worship.

Indeed, each of the elements of Lutheran worship shapes and prepares us to seek justice in our world. In the Lutheran rite of baptism, the baptized is given the solemn vocation "to strive for justice in all the world." In Holy Communion, we are formed to be a community that bears one another up and shoulders each other's burdens. Worship is both intrinsically good as an expression of our devotion to God and instrumentally good, inasmuch as it forms us to be the people of God the rest of the week.

It is for this reason that Lindberg argues "worship and welfare are inseparable."[28] Quoting Luther, Lindberg calls social ethics—our moral action as members of a community in service of our neighbors, including our economic behavior—the "liturgy after the liturgy."[29] Rhee similarly points out that in the early church, "the role and authority of clergy (especially bishops as 'lovers of the poor') was unequivocally defined by not only their liturgical/sacramental ('spiritual') function but also their social ('material') function of spearheading and operating extensive services and charities for the poor, the infirm, the elderly, the disabled, and the helpless."[30] The "unwarranted and unfortunate wedge between these 'spiritual' and 'social' ministries of churches . . . is a concept foreign to early Christianity" and, indeed, to the Reformation, too.[31]

In comparing worship and service, Torvend argues, "To ask the question, 'which is more important, worship or welfare?' is the same as asking, 'which is more important, breathing in or breathing out?'"[32] For Lutherans, there is no separation between word and sacrament and word and service. This isn't a matter of needing to do good works to get our worship up to snuff. Rather, it is recognition that both worship and service are part of our formation. Encountering our neighbors, accompanying one another, and building relationships in our communities through ministry forms us as a people better equipped to understand both the ways God works in the world and our continual need for grace as we walk together down roads marred by complex and entrenched injustice. Worship and service are inseparable expressions of a single ecclesial identity.

Putting It in Practice

How do these insights shape ministry practically? Here are some suggestions, though this list is far from exhaustive. Hopefully, the essays here and the discussion generated by the questions at the end of this book can help guide your congregation toward other practical steps.

1) Ask the hard questions.

Lutherans involved in anti-hunger ministries are uniquely situated to start asking hard questions about the causes of hunger in our communities. Lindberg puts it well and is worth quoting at length:

> So we see these neighbors in need around us, these kids...
> who economically cannot afford a backpack so we fill them
> with pencils and we give them this good stuff, that's great!
> Now, what if we also said, "Maybe we should try to work
> on helping their parents get $15 per hour [for their work]."

Not that we want to stop giving them backpacks anymore, but maybe they could actually afford to get backpacks if we had a more just economic job situation. When you move beyond charity to social justice issues, systemic issues, then the cost becomes a lot more evident.[33]

Asking the hard questions means being willing to listen to challenging answers. It demands openness to critiques of the system that will call us deeper into activism and advocacy. It is also one of the reasons advocacy and community organizing are such critical parts of the work of ELCA World Hunger. The relief and development programs supported by the ELCA are vital ministries in local communities, but advocacy and community organizing are intentionally directed at the types of changes that may eventually make relief ministries (thankfully) obsolete.

This also means asking hard questions about our own service. Does our ministry engage in justice-seeking, even as it provides for immediate relief? How might our work be more comprehensive and meet deeper needs? One way to examine these questions is to look at reporting. So often, most ministries report the numbers of meals served or the number of clients helped. This is great information that points to the prevalence of need in a community, but it isn't impact. Instead of asking how much or how many were served, we need to start looking more closely at whether our ministry is actually moving the needle on the rates of hunger and poverty locally and nationally. This is where the answers may be harder to face.

2) Offer an alternative vision.

Another ministry supported by ELCA World Hunger provides a good example of an alternative vision for ministry. One of their participants, Kenneth, fits the stereotype that so many people have in mind when they think of people living in poverty. He was a convicted criminal. He was a former drug user. He was unemployed. His choices were, in some ways, exactly what many supporters of the merit-based economy look at when explaining and justifying his unemployment. But the people of Cross Lutheran Church in Milwaukee, Wisconsin, brought a different lens to their work with Kenneth. When he took part in their jobs program, they saw him as a person of worth, as someone with skills and talents to contribute, and, importantly, as someone they would accompany as he sought work.

The church's jobs program is not just a social ministry. It is a testimony to an economy that offers more than just rewards and punishments. If it is a matter of merit, then Kenneth and their other clients "deserve" the opportunity to contribute to and share in the benefits of the economy by virtue of their being human beings made in the image of God and gifted with contributions to make to the community. The work of Cross's jobs program reflects the alternative economic witness discernable from our shared Lutheran heritage. It is a witness that demands we look deeply into our current economy, identify its shortcomings, and offer an alternative vision to the status quo. Learning more about current economic realities is the first step. But if Lutherans are to be the "leaven" that Helen Rhee suggests, then this alternative economic witness must be embodied in our ministries, from the food pantry to the jobs program and everything in between. Moreover, this economic witness must shape the public face of the Lutheran church. Compassion is important, but public expressions of compassion or sympathy in the face of economic or social crisis must also be informed by an alternative witness for justice that clearly names why some of us are more vulnerable to crises than others.

3) Worship **and** serve.

Worship forms us for service, and service forms us for worship. The awareness of our dependence on God that brings us to the altar of Holy Communion, the knowledge of our sinful shortcomings that draws from us our confession, and the deep understanding of need that elicits our prayers all become richer when they are informed by experiences as servants and neighbors in our community. As we distribute food from a pantry, participate in educational programs, or advocate for fair economic policies, we must recognize that this is church. This is part of what it means to be the people of God, and it is equally crucial to our identity as Word and Sacrament is on Sunday mornings. This doesn't mean that we try to convert clients into members. But it does mean that if this side of ministry is missing, we are no more "church" than if there were no Bible, bread, or wine in our sanctuary. The church is most fully church with both a common chest and a common meal. To separate the two, to believe we can be fully church with merely word and sacrament absent authentic service of the neighbor, is to lose our identity.

4) Employ a triple-bottom line.

Pahl, in his essay above, describes the three goods of a "triple-bottom line": people, planet, and profits. This can be an instructive guide for anti-hunger ministries, too. Of course, anti-hunger ministries aren't focused on "profits" per se, but finances and budgets are part of their everyday reality. On the one hand, ministries must be conscious of their own financial circumstances. Ministry takes money, and no supporter wants their donation misused. On the other hand, it is easy to slide from this into a mindset of scarcity and to focus on the limits we must face rather than the opportunities we can embrace. This places solvency above authenticity. We see this in the difference between hunger relief that strictly limits clients in varieties of ways and hunger relief that strives to empower clients within practical limits.

At Crescent City Café in New Orleans, Louisiana, guests are served a community meal in a space finely equipped with white tablecloths and real (non-disposable) tableware. Guests are greeted by a host and seated at tables to dine. This is not the most economically efficient model for food distribution, but it is a challenge to the more traditional model of a soup kitchen—a model the founders of the café intentionally sought to avoid. The café may never be able to serve the sheer quantity of meals distributed by traditional models, but that isn't their goal. Rather, their goal is to create a space where guests feel treated with dignity and where community can be nurtured.

This is what is meant by incorporating people as part of a "triple-bottom line." How we measure impact moves from the number of people served to the good the ministry accomplishes and the impact it has in building community. For Lutherans, this is measured not in pounds but in the quality of community God creates with human hands through our ministry. This might mean shifting how we understand our goals, away from responding to a problem and toward responding to people.

In reflecting on Jesus' admonition to the disciples that "the poor will always be with you," Luther countered, "but constant care should be taken that, since these evils are always in evidence, they are always opposed."[34] The Lutheran heritage embodies a "Protest"-ant tradition, one richly colored by a faith that brings into relationship people at the margins and in the center, people who have been excluded by economic forces and people who have benefitted from them. These relationships call us toward an alternative witness, one that refuses complacency in the face of injustice. This heritage calls and equips us to recognize injustice, to refuse to "call evil good," and to do something about it. It is a challenging heritage that moves us from responding to hunger and poverty to effective, authentic action that can end it. And it is a heritage that assures us this, too, is part of professing the Good News— declaring that another world is possible, a world in which the common good is truly common. Perfection may be beyond us in this world, but the Lutheran witness is a firm declaration that fairness and justice are not out of reach, nor is a world in which all are fed.

Endnotes

1 Arne Johan Vetleson, *Perception, Empathy, and Judgment: An Inquiry into the Preconditions of Moral Performance* (University Park, Pennsylvania: The Pennsylvania State University Press, 1993).

2 James M. Childs, "On Seeing Ourselves: Anthropology and Social Ethics," *Word & World* 7/1 (1982): 229.

3 Ibid. See also Bruce Birch and Larry Rasmussen, *The Predicament of the Prosperous* (Philadelphia: Westminster, 1978), cited in ibid.

4 "Welfare" in the United States typically refers to the means-tested cash benefit program Aid to Families with Dependent Children (AFDC). This program, unlike programs that provide in-kind benefits or benefits that can only be used in particularly ways such as to purchase food, provided parents and guardians in poverty with cash they could use to meet their varying needs.

5 Laurie MacLeod, Darrel Montero, Darrel, and Alan Speer, "America's Changing Attitudes Toward Welfare and Welfare Recipients,1938-1995,"*The Journal of Sociology & Social Welfare* 26/2(2015): 179.

6 Ibid, 178.

7 Ibid, 185.

8 In New Jersey, where the Lutheran Episcopal Advocacy Ministry of New Jersey (LEAMNJ) is active in a movement for paid sick leave, nearly one in three employees have no paid time off for illness. This leaves them vulnerable to lost wages and lost employment when medical emergencies arise.

9 The US Census Bureau estimates that, in 2014, medical expenses added about 3.5 percentage points to the rate of poverty in the United States. In 2014, 15.3 percent of Americans were living in poverty. If not for out-of-pocket medical expenses, this would be 11.8 percent. See U.S. Census Bureau, "The Supplemental Poverty Level: 2014," published September 2015. Available at www.census.gov.

10 The economic prospects of citizens returning from incarceration are bleak. Research indicates that people who have been incarcerated are less likely to find stable employment and will earn up to 40 percent less money over the course of their lifetimes than people who have never been incarcerated. See for example Bruce Western, "The Impact of Incarceration on Wage Mobility and Inequality,"

American Sociological Review 67 (2002): 526-546; The Pew Charitable Trusts, *Collateral Costs: Incarceration's Effect on Economic Mobility.* Washington, D.C., 2010.

11 A 2015 report from Harvard University's Joint Center for Housing Studies found that 21.3 million Americans were "cost-burdened" renters, meaning they spent more than 30 percent of their income on housing. The study notes that, from 2001 to 2014, average rent rose 7 percent while household income fell 9 percent. This makes it particularly difficult for low-income households to make ends meet and plan for unexpected events. The full report is available at http://www.jchs.harvard.edu/research/publications/americas-rental-housing-expanding-options-diverse-and-growing-demand.

12 SNAP stands for Supplemental Nutrition Assistance Program, a federal program administered by states that provides benefits to recipients to purchase food items. This program is what many refer to as "food stamps."

13 Robert D. Lupton, *Toxic Charity: How Churches and Charities Hurt Those They Help* (New York: Harper One, 2011); Steve Corbett and Brian Fikkert, *When Helping Hurts: How to Alleviate Poverty without Hurting the Poor . . . and Yourself* (Chicago: Moody, 2012).

14 This definition is based in part on Rehman Sobhan, *Challenging the Injustice of Poverty: Agendas for Inclusive Development in South Asia* (New Delhi: Sage, 2010).

15 William T. Cavanaugh, *Being Consumed: Economics and Christian Desire* (Grand Rapids, Michigan: Wm B. Eerdmans Publishing Co., Inc., 2008), 96.

16 World Economic Forum, "Outlook on the Global Agenda 2015," available at http://reports.weforum.org/outlook-global-agenda-2015/top-10-trends-of-2015/1-deepening-income-inequality/. Accessed 17 March, 2016.

17 See U.S. Census Bureau, "Income and Poverty in the United States: 2014" (September 2015), available at http://www.census.gov/content/dam/Census/library/publications/2015/demo/p60-252.pdf; USDA, Alisha Coleman-Jensen, Matthew P. Rabbitt, Christian Gregory, and Anita Singh. *Household Food Security in the United States in 2014*, ERR-194, U.S. Department of Agriculture, Economic Research Service, September 2015; FAO, IFAD, and WFP, The State of Food Insecurity in the World 2015: Meeting the 2015 International Hunger Targets—Taking Stock of Uneven Progress (Rome: FAO, 2015); Nicholas Fitz, "Economic Inequality: It's Far Worse than You Think," Scientific American (March 2015), http://www.scientificamerican.com/article/economic-inequality-it-s-far-worse-than-you-think/; and Drew Desilver, "For Most Workers, Real Wages Barely Budged for Decades," Pew Research Center website (October 2014), http://www.pewresearch.org/fact-tank/2014/10/09/for-most-workers-real-wages-have-barely-budged-for-decades/.

18 Samuel Torvend, interview with author, November 7, 2015.

19 Gordon Huffman, interview with author, November 7, 2015.

20 In a 2004 article published in the *Journal of Poverty*, Lisa D. Brush found a "clear association" between vulnerability to abuse and vulnerability to poverty. Women who experienced intimate partner violence earned less money, had more difficulty paying bills, and experienced slightly higher rates of food

insecurity than women who did not. Brush also found that, for some women, the violence they experienced from intimate partners was specifically related to work. This "work-related violence" included physical beatings, threats, and physical restraint from going to work. As is often the case, control, domination, and abuse weren't limited to overt violence, however. Intimate partners also sabotaged women's efforts to work by failing to show up for childcare, stealing cars or keys, or behaving inappropriately at the woman's place of work. See Lisa D. Brush, "Battering and the Poverty Trap," *Journal of Poverty* 8,3 (2004): 23-43. See also, Ryan P. Cumming, "Intimate Partner Violence: A Hunger Issue, ELCA World Hunger blog, June 2, 2014, http://blogs.elca.org/worldhunger/intimate-partner-violence-a-hunger-issue/.

21 Helen Rhee, *Loving the Poor, Saving the Rich: Wealth, Poverty, and Early Christian Formation* (Grand Rapids, Michigan: Baker Academic, 2012), 210.

22 Ibid, 210, quoting Douglas A. Hicks.

23 Torvend, interview.

24 Lindberg essay in this volume.

25 Torvend, interview.

26 Lindberg in this volume.

27 Antonia Blumberg, "Shobi's Table Is the Free Food Truck that Every City Needs," *Huffington Post*, September 7, 2014, http://www.huffingtonpost.com/2014/09/07/shobis-table-food-truck-ministry_n_5700769.html.

28 Lindberg in this volume.

29 Ibid.

30 Rhee, 204.

31 Ibid, 204-205.

32 Torvend, interview.

33 Carter Lindberg, interview with the author, November 7, 2015.

34 Lindberg essay here, quoting Luther.

Discussion Questions

Luther and the Common Chest
Carter Lindberg

1. Read Isaiah 58:5-9a. What does the writer of Isaiah consider "true" fasting that is pleasing to God? How is this different from the type of fasting we talk about most often in church?

2. What is your personal story of experiencing God's love? How do this story and your faith shape your service of others?

3. Martin Luther's "frank speech" from the pulpit challenged his congregation to be more generous in their support of the common chest. When have you felt challenged by "frank speech" in a sermon, presentation, workshop, etc.? How did this encourage you to take action later on? What are the obstacles to "frank speech" about generosity in churches today? How might these be overcome?

4. Support for the Common Chests came from a variety of sources, including donations from churchgoers. This support was framed as an expression of Lutheran beliefs about both charity and justice. Consider your own stewardship of financial resources. How does or how might your stewardship reflect a concern for justice and fairness? How can giving be considered as something more than charity?

5. As Lindberg writes, the town of Leisnig elected four stewards based on their knowledge and abilities to distribute loans and gifts from the common chest according to the need of the recipients. Who would the "four stewards" be today? What factors might they have to consider to determine need?

6. Lindberg quotes Brazilian Catholic Archbishop Dom Helder Camara: "When I give food to the poor, they call me a saint. When I ask why the poor have no food, they call me a Communist." What contrast is Archbishop Camara making? What is he saying about

the difference between charity (giving food) and justice (asking why people in poverty have no food)? Is his quote still relevant today?

7. Luther claimed that the Catholic Church of his day was contributing to poverty by selling indulgences to the poor and by making a life of poverty seem romantic or holy. In what ways might people of faith still be contributing to the growth of poverty? In what ways does the church work against poverty?

8. One of Luther's critiques of the church in his day was that it claimed to offer salvation to people if they bought indulgences or contributed money to charity. This was starkly different from the free gift of salvation Luther found in scripture. How might modern appeals to charity in our own time contribute to a notion that salvation can be purchased or that charity can atone for sins like greed? Does Luther's understanding of salvation call the modern church to deeper activism in response to hunger and poverty?

9. Luther lifts up the close ties between worship and social action by referring to social ethics as the "liturgy after the liturgy." How does worship in your congregation inspire concern for problems outside the church, for example, poverty, hunger, conflict, or homelessness? Consider ways that these social concerns might be lifted up in the parts of worship: confession and forgiveness, hymns, prayers, litanies, sacraments, etc.

"Greed Is an Unbelieving Scoundrel"
Samuel Torvend

1. Read Jeremiah 22:13-17
   a. How does greed work against God's desire for the people?
   b. What would an economy based on God's desire for the world look like?
   c. What practical steps can the church take toward this new economy?

2. How do you experience the tension between the tendency to take care of yourself and the call of the Gospel to live for others? What lessons from Scripture or your own faith experiences help you balance these?

3. How is greed connected to unbelief or idolatry? How does a greedy pursuit of "more"—more wealth, more power, more possessions—turn us away from God?

4. In what ways can "Christian love that helps and serves the needy" offer an alternative to greed?

5. What might be some modern forms of the common chest established in Leisnig? How do these—or how might these—"Common Chests" not only respond to poverty but also prevent it?

6. What does Luther see as the purpose of government? How does this differ from other "purposes" toward which civic leaders might be drawn?

7. How can a modern church, so distant from its past, recover the economic insights of theologians from Christian history? Are these early Christians still relevant today?

8. How might church leaders address the challenge of balancing prophetic critique of greed with equally compelling hope for those eager for practical change?

9. What does Torvend see as the greatest challenges for the church in addressing modern economic injustice? Do you agree with him? How might these and other challenges be met?

10. Torvend draws a connection between the general tendency each individual has to think only of themselves and laws or policies that harm those who are in need. What are some examples of this connection between personal greed and economic injustice? How might the Church help change some of the ways greed influences laws or policies?

The Subversive Luther
Cynthia Moe-Lobeda

1. Read Amos 5:10-15.

   a. What are the transgressions of the people of Israel?

   b. What reasons are given for their punishment?

   c. How does God call them to live instead? (Note: In ancient Israel, "the gate" was the setting for civil and criminal courts. Thus, Amos is most likely referring to injustice in the court system.)

2. What does it mean for you to experience salvation as God's free gift? How does this shape your choices as a neighbor? As a worker or employer? As a citizen? As an investor? As someone living in poverty?

3. Consider recent news reports about people living in poverty. How are they portrayed? What reasons, if any, are given for their poverty?

How does this view of people living in poverty compare to the view of people in poverty we have as Christians?

4. Think of a time when you witnessed or learned about an incident of civil disobedience. Were you in support of it? Why or why not? What is the difference between the kind of disobedience Moe-Lobeda describes and mere law-breaking? What might be an occasion for a congregation to engage in civil disobedience in service of your neighbors?

5. According to the author, Luther defines sin in three related ways:

   a. The self turned in upon itself

   b. The human tendency to do everything to promote ourselves or out of concern for ourselves

   c. Treating resources as if they are our own, rather than gifts of God

   Which definition resonates with you the most? How do you see this kind of sin working in our economy and politics? How might the church—or how *does* the church—respond with an alternative?

6. How does the poverty of Luther's day compare to poverty in our own time? What remedies can people of faith provide by accompanying people in poverty?

7. Make a list of the possible causes of poverty and hunger. Try to write down as many as possible. Which of these causes are within the control of someone living in poverty or hunger? Which are outside of their control? Which of the causes are in *our* control?

8. What risks do congregations face in embracing the "unsafe," "subversive" faces of Lutheran beliefs? What opportunities for growth or renewal might these faces hold for congregations?

9. What does it mean to be a "rusty tool" of God's? Discuss together the significance of both words—"rusty" and "tool."

10. What does it mean for pastors to "unmask hidden injustice"? What injustices do you think often go unnoticed? Is this responsibility limited only to pastors?

An Economic Reading of Luther's Catechisms in Long Context
John Pahl

1. Pahl links salvation to an experience of freedom in politics, economics, and social service. Do you experience salvation as "freedom"? How? What does your salvation—however you

understand it, have to do with who you are as a citizen? As a participant in the economy?

2. What economic behaviors does Pahl draw from Luther's interpretation of the Ten Commandments? How faithful has the church been in fostering these behaviors? Can you give concrete examples of how the church has been faithful to, or failed to be faithful to, the kind of economic behaviors Pahl sees in Luther's interpretation of the Ten Commandments in the catechisms?

3. Are you familiar with the way Northern European Lutherans have applied Luther's economic teachings—as Pahl suggests? What might American Lutherans learn from these examples, if anything?

4. Are you familiar with Lutheran social ministry organizations as an expression of the church's work? Do you think these agencies have put into practice any of the economic teachings in Luther's catechisms, as Pahl suggests? Can you give concrete examples from your relationships or work with these agencies?

5. When have you felt blessed by the economy? When have you felt cursed by it? In less than five words, describe your experiences of the economy where you live. Do these experiences help you see the economy as working for the benefit of all? Why or why not?

6. What does an economy based on Lutheran teachings look like? How can the church be part of making this a reality?

7. Lutherans have a long history of action related to service of people facing hunger and poverty. Where do you see this action happening in the Lutheran church today? How can this service be an alternative to an economy that is marked by inequality and injustice?

8. How might you incorporate economics in your ministry? In faith formation at your ministry site?

9. Economics was a central concern for Luther when he wrote the Catechisms that were used to train new Lutherans. How might your congregation help new and not-so-new members see the economic implications of Lutheran faith?

10. In a time when many churches must focus on raising enough money to stay open, how does your church continue to express a "triple bottom line" focus on people, the planet, and profits?

Luther: Forgotten, But Not Gone
Tim Huffman

1. We learn from this chapter that Luther's life ended where it began, among workers in the copper mines of Mansfield, Germany. Yet he was a theologian, not a miner; a teacher, not an economist; a preacher, not a politician. In the discussion on how to eliminate poverty and hunger, what is the proper role of the economist? The politician? The preacher?

2. Luther felt that before the church expressed judgment against unjust economic practices or corruption in politics, it needed to address God's word of judgment on the life of the church itself. What are some of the ways that the church has participated (or participates) in injustice? How might the church correct these shortcomings?

3. Huffman's basic argument is that many theologians have found in Luther's work themes of liberation and justice. Where in your faith do you feel called to work for justice and liberation of others? When have you felt liberated yourself?

4. Luther decried the popular belief that people who are wealthy are *morally* better than those who are poor. Was he correct? Why do you think this belief continues to be popular today?

5. Huffman says that we can re-energize our Reformation heritage if we "situate political debates and economic decisions in a theological and ethical context." What do you think he means by this? How can this happen without confusing God's word with a current political or economic notion?

6. Huffman implies that Pope Francis might be close to Martin Luther when it comes to addressing God's word to the *systemic* causes of economic injustice. If this is accurate, how might Lutherans and Catholics work together to correct injustice?

Suggestions for Further Reading

Reference Works

Timothy Wengert, ed., *Dictionary of Luther and the Lutheran Tradition* (Grand Rapids, Michigan: Baker Academic Books, 2016).

Robert Kolb, Irene Dingel, and L'Ubomir Batka, eds., *The Oxford Handbook of Martin Luther's Theology* (New York: Oxford University Press, 2014).

Paul Hinlicky and Derek Nelson, eds., *The Oxford Encyclopedia of Martin Luther*, 2 vols., (New York: Oxford University Press, 2017).

Books and Articles

Walter Altmann, *Luther and Liberation: A Latin American Perspective*, 2nd ed. (Minneapolis: Fortress Press, 2016).

Paul Chung, Ulrich Duchrow, and Craig Nesson, *Liberating Lutheran Theology: Freedom for Justice and Solidarity in Global Context* (Minneapolis: Fortress Press, 2011).

Ulrich Duchrow and Carsten Jochum-Bortfeld, eds., *Liberation toward Justice/Befreiung zur Gerechtigkeit* (Berlin: LIT Verlag, 2015).

Ulrich Duchrow and Hans Urlich, eds., *Befreiung vom Mammon/ Liberation from Mammon* (Berlin: LIT Verlag, 2015).

Ulrich Duchrow and Martin Hoffmann, eds., *Politik und Ökonomie der Befreiung/Politics and Economics of Liberation* (Berlin: LIT Verlag, 2015).

Ulrich Duchrow and Craig Nessan, eds., *Befreiung von Gewalt zum Leben in Frieden/Liberation from Violence for Life in Peace* (Berlin: LIT Verlag, 2015).

Ulrich Duchrow and Karen Bloomquist, eds., *Kirche—befreit zu Widerstand und Transformation/Church—Liberated for Resistance and Transformation* (Berlin: LIT Verlag, 2015).

Barbara Ehrenreich, *This Land is Their Land: Reports from a Divided Nation* (New York: Henry Holt, 2008).

George W. Forell, *Faith Active in Love: An Investigation of the Principles Underlying Luther's Social Ethics* (Eugene, Oregon: Wipf & Stock, 1999; reprint from Minneapolis: Augsburg Publishing House, 1954).

Gustavo Gutierrez, *A Theology of Liberation: 15th Anniversary Edition* (Maryknoll, New York: Orbis Books, 1988).

Berndt Hamm, "Martin Luther's Revolutionary Theology of Pure Gift Without Reciprocation," *Lutheran Quarterly* 29/2 (2015): 125-161.

Ada Maria Isasi-Diaz, *Mujerista Theology: A Theology for the Twenty-First Century* (Maryknoll, New York: Orbis Books, 1996).

Carter Lindberg, *Beyond Charity: Reformation Initiatives for the Poor* (Minneapolis: Fortress Press, 1993).

Carter Lindberg, "Luther on Wall Street and Welfare," *Logia: A Journal of Lutheran Theology* 23/4 (2014): 7-12.

Foster R. McCurley, ed., *Social Ministry in the Lutheran Tradition* (Minneapolis: Fortress, 2008).

Cynthia Moe-Lobeda, *Healing A Broken World: Globalization and God* (Minneapolis: Fortress Press, 2002).

Cynthia Moe-Lobeda, *Resisting Structural Evil: Love as Ecological-Economic Vocation* (Minneapolis: Fortress Press, 2013).

Cynthia Moe-Lobeda, *Public Church: For the Life of the World* (Minneapolis: Fortress Press, 2004).

Jon Pahl, *Empire of Sacrifice: The Religious Origins of American Violence* (New York: New York University Press, 2012).

Albrecht Peters, *Commentary on Luther's Catechisms: Ten Commandments (*St. Louis: Concordia Publishing House, 2009)

Larry Rasmussen, *Earth Honoring Faith: Religious Ethics in a New Key* (New York: Oxford University Press, 2014).

Robert Reich, *Inequality for All* (documentary film and website).

Ricardo Reith, "Luther on Greed" in Timothy Wengert, ed., *Harvesting Martin*

Luther's Reflections on Theology, Ethics, and the Church (Grand Rapids: Wm. B. Eerdmans Publishing Co., 2004).

Brooks Schramm and Kirsi Stjerna, eds., *Martin Luther, the Bible, and the Jewish People: A Reader* (Minneapolis: Fortress Press, 2012).

Jon Sobrino, *No Salvation Outside the Poor: Prophetic-Utopian Essays* (Maryknoll, New York: Orbis Books, 2008).

Elsa Tamez, *The Amnesty of Grace: Justification by Faith from a Latin American Perspective* (Nashville: Abingdon Press, 1993).

Samuel Torvend, "Common Property for All Who Are Needy: Eucharistic Practice in the Midst of Economic Injustice" in Ulrich Duchrow and Martin Hoffmann, eds., *Politics and Economics of Liberation* (Berlin: LIT Verlag, 2015).

Samuel Torvend, *Luther and the Hungry Poor: Gathered Fragments* (Minneapolis: Fortress Press, 2008).

Paul Wee, "Reclaiming Luther's Forgotten Economic Reforms," *Lutheran Forum* 48/1(2014): 52-56.

Notes on Contributors

Dr. Carter Lindberg is Professor Emeritus of Church History at Boston University School of Theology. His book, *Beyond Charity, Reformation Initiatives for the Poor* (Fortress, 1993) has been instrumental in raising awareness of Martin Luther's writings about economic justice. Among his publications are *Love: A Brief History* (2008), *A Brief History of Christianity* (2005), *The Pietist Theologians* (2004), *The Reformation Theologians* (2001), and *The European Reformations* (2nd ed., 2010), all published by Wiley-Blackwell.

Dr. Cynthia Moe-Lobeda is a well-known Lutheran ethicist and is Professor of Theological and Social Ethics at Pacific Lutheran Theological Seminary. She has lectured or consulted in Africa, Asia, Europe, Latin America, and many parts of North America in theological ethics addressing matters of economic globalization, moral agency and hope, public church, faith-based resistance to systemic injustice, climate justice as related to race and class, and ethical implications of resurrection and incarnation. Among her books are *Healing a Broken World: Globalization and God* (Fortress, 2002), *Public Church: For the Life of the World* (Fortress, 2004), and *Resisting Structural Evil: Love as Ecological-Economic Vocation* (Fortress, 2013).

Dr. Samuel Torvend holds the University Chair in Lutheran Studies at Pacific Lutheran University (PLU) in Tacoma, Washington. He is an active participant in the Radicalizing Reformation Project and has published on the relationship between Luther's sacramental and economic reforms. At PLU, he teaches courses on Reformation history, Lutheran political commitments, and the history of social ethics, in particular Luther's reform of social welfare. Among his books are *Flowing Water, Uncommon Birth: Christian Baptism in a Post-Christian Culture* (Fortress, 2011), *Luther and the Hungry Poor: Gathered Fragments* (Fortress, 2008), and *Daily Bread, Holy Meal: Opening the Gifts of Holy Communion* (Augsburg Fortress, 2004).

Dr. Jon Pahl is Peter Paul and Elizabeth Hagan Professor in the History of Christianity at the Lutheran Theological Seminary at Philadelphia (LTSP). He has enjoyed speaking with congregations and audiences from Ankara, Turkey, to Anaheim, California. As a social justice activist, Pahl founded the campus chapter of Habitat for Humanity at Valparaiso University, served on the board of directors at Lutheran Settlement House in Philadelphia, and now chairs the Board of Feast of Justice—a hunger ministry in northeast Philadelphia. Jon is also the chief architect of the MAPL (Master of Arts in Public Leadership) degree program at LTSP that prepares future leaders of social ministry organizations. Among his writings are *Paradox Lost: Free Will and Political Liberty in American Culture, 1630-1760*; *Shopping Malls and Other Sacred Spaces: Putting God in Place*; and, most recently, *Empire of Sacrifice: The Religious Origins of American Violence* (NYU Press).

Dr. Gordon "Tim" Huffman recently retired as the John H. F. Kuder Professor of Christian Mission at Trinity Lutheran Seminary in Columbus, Ohio, where he also served as editor of the *Trinity Seminary Review*. According to Huffman, "Economics, politics, and sociology are at the very center of the theological task. Not to understand them and their role in the societies around the world guarantees inadequate theology." Among his writings: *The Lutheran Confessions: A Digital Anthology* (31 pages on CD-ROM, Kindle, Nook, iPhone, iPod touch, interactive teaching resource, 2011), "The Confessions and Mission," *Trinity Seminary Review*, Winter/Spring 2012.

Dr. Ryan Cumming is Program Director for Hunger Education with the Evangelical Lutheran Church in America. As an academic, he teaches courses on religion, theology, and ethics at universities in Illinois and Michigan and enjoys presenting for congregations and scholarly audiences. In addition to writings on hunger, poverty, and social justice available in print and online, he is the author of *The African American Challenge to Just War Theory: A Christian Approach* (Palgrave Macmillan, 2013).

Dr. Paul Wee, a pastor of the Evangelical Lutheran Church in America, has been adjunct professor at the Elliott School of International Affairs at George Washington University. He served as assistant general secretary for International Affairs and Human Rights of the Geneva-based Lutheran World Federation and as International Theological Director of the Luther Center in Wittenberg, Germany.

He was program officer in the Religion and Peacemaking unit of the United Sates Institute of Peace, working primarily on interfaith conflict resolution in Nigeria and Colombia. He is author of *American Destiny and the Calling of the Church* (Augsburg Fortress, 2006).